MAKING A HOME FOR FAITH

NURTURING THE SPIRITUAL LIFE OF YOUR CHILDREN

ELIZABETH F. CALDWELL

The Pilgrim Press

Cleveland, Ohio

The Pilgrim Press, Cleveland, Ohio 44115
© 2000 by Elizabeth F. Caldwell

Grateful acknowledgment to the following for permission to reprint material in this book: From Discovering the Bible with Children, Teacher's Resource Book, vol. 5, no. 1, p. 2. Used by permission of Curriculum Publishing, Congregational Ministries Division, Presbyterian Church (U.S.A.), 100 Witherspoon St., Louisville KY 40202. • From "Child of Blessing, Child of Promise," text © 1981 by Ronald S. Cole-Turner. All rights reserved. Used by permission. • From "'Is This Nativity?' Elementary Fellowship Visits Second Harvest Food Bank," Second Story, newsletter of Second Presbyterian Church, Nashville, Tennessee, January 1997. • Faith statements in Appendix 1 used by permission of Kirsten Stangenes and Allison Denny, members of Lincoln Park Presbyterian Church, Chicago, Illinois.

Biblical quotations, unless otherwise noted, are from the New Revised Standard Version of the Bible, © 1989 by the Division of Christian Education of the National Council of Churches of Christ in the U.S.A., and are used by permission. Adaptations have been made for inclusivity.

Printed in the United States of America on acid-free paper

05   04   03   5   4

Library of Congress Cataloging-in-Publication Data

Caldwell, Elizabeth, 1948–
    Making a home for faith : nurturing the spiritual life of your children / Elizabeth F. Caldwell.
        p. cm.
    Includes bibliographical references.
    ISBN 0-8298-1370-5 (paper : alk. paper)
    1. Christian education of children.   2. Children—Religious life.
3. Parenting—Religious aspects—Christianity.   I. Title.

BV1475.2 .C315 2000
248.8'45—dc21
                                                        99-057653

CONTENTS

Preface . . . v

Acknowledgments . . . x

1
A Halo, a Star, and a Bathrobe: Making a Home for Faith . . . 1

2
Parenting for Faith Expression . . . 12

3
Imprints of Faith . . . 29

4
"And When Your Child Asks" . . . 47

5
A Faithful Ecology at Home, at Church, and in the World . . . 72

6
Where Do I Go for More Help? . . . 97

APPENDIX 1
Faith Statements . . . 107

APPENDIX 2
Guide for Completing the Faith Statement . . . 109

APPENDIX 3
Learning to Become Storytellers . . . 110

Notes   111

- "When my child asks about God, where do I begin?"
- "My daughter has friends of other faiths in her class, and she wonders why we are Christian. What do I say?"
- "The Bible is full of many difficult concepts. I know I don't understand them. How do I begin to read the Bible with my son?"
- "I need to be honest with you. I really don't know much about the Bible. I stopped going to church when I was a teenager. Now I've started coming back because I want my children to have this experience. You teach them about God and the Bible because I don't know enough."
- "There are so many resources in bookstores and on the Web, ones I think might be helpful as I think about my own life of faith and that of my child. What criteria do I use in making my selections?"

Many parents are searching for ways to nurture their children in the life of the Christian faith. They come with honest questions and look to the church for answers. Others, realizing their lack of biblical and theological background, turn their children over to the church and the church school—the professionals, so to speak—because they want it done right, by the experts. Still other adults, realizing that they have more questions about faith than they have answers, wonder what kind of help they can be to their religiously curious children. Perhaps one of these descriptions fits you or someone you know in your church or in your community.

This book has grown out of conversations, teaching, and reflection with adults who are asking questions like the ones at the beginning of this preface. In listening to the concerns and questions of parents, I hear confessions of inadequacy, requests for answers to specific questions asked by a child, and sincere requests for help: How do I begin to talk about faith with my child? I also hear wonderful stories of children's conversations about God, their affirmations, wonderings, and questions, and parents who are able to listen and feel comfortable with their responses.

In many faith traditions, parents present their infants in worship for the sacrament of infant baptism or dedication. At that moment, parents affirm their commitments to the living of the Christian faith. And then in the midst of public worship, a parent promises, with the help and support of everyone in the congregation, to raise her child in the life of the Christian faith. A hymn may be sung:

> Child of blessing, child of promise,
> Baptized with the Spirit's sign,
> With this water God has sealed you
> Unto love and grace divine.[1]

If there is a baptism, waters from the font drip down the child's face, marking her forever for a life begun in faith. Prayers for the child and her family are offered, and sometimes a gift is given, a baptismal candle to be lit each year on the anniversary or a Bible storybook so the child can hear the stories of God's faithful people in the Bible. At the conclusion, the whole congregation celebrates the life of the newest one joined in the body of Christ.

In an earlier book, *Come Unto Me: Rethinking the Sacraments for Children,* I explored the meaning of baptism and Eucharist for children, parents, and congregations. Rather than being momentary events in our lives, the sacraments have meaning for our daily living as God's faithful people. In that book I suggested ways that congregations could prepare parents who were bringing their children for baptism.

Since writing that book, I have grown increasingly concerned with how often our churches assume that parents know what to do with their children in regard to nurturing them in a life of faith. What happens after baptism or dedication concerns me and is the focus of this book. After the announcement of adoption or birth, a baptism or dedication, some children are brought back to the church on a regular basis by their parents, and they are nurtured in the life of the faithful congregation. Other children are never seen again by the congregation. What happens during the in-between time, that formative space of life between adoption by or birth into a family and the public confession of faith as a youth at confirmation or baptism?

There is a lot of time between these faithful marker events. Children who grow up involved with their families in a congregation experience the life of faith in words, music, stories, worship, educational activities, and faithful acts of service and witness. One to three hours a week on Sunday or a weekday are essential, formative moments for children to learn and experience the meaning and reality of living the Christian faith.

Yet children also live in a society that is increasingly and wonderfully diverse in culture and faith traditions. The time between church school, worship, and midweek learning opportunities becomes critical in nurturing children in the Christian faith. And the parent or parents—and sometimes the extended family of grandparents, aunts, uncles, or godparents—are essential conversation partners with children and young persons as they articulate questions of faith and struggle to make sense of the connections between biblical stories and faithful living in the world.

Who or what prepares us for this opportunity and responsibility to nurture someone else in growing in a life of faith? Is there a basic amount of knowledge we need? What are the ABCs of "parenting for faith expression"?[2] What if we make a serious mistake? What if our children discover we don't have all the answers?

I believe that if a parent is active in the life of a congregation, is committed to nurturing her or his spiritual life, and is willing to struggle with questions of faith and life and the mysteries of God, she or he will be able to be the kind of parent who enables a child to grow in faith. It is that simple and that complex. It requires commitment, trust, action, silence, and listening. Equally essential is an affirmation of faithful confidence.

Parenting skills evolve over time as family members mature together. Mistakes are made, and vows are uttered, "I'll never do that or say that again." Learnings are reinforced about what works and what doesn't work with a particular child. This is also true for the parent who seeks to help a child grow in Christian faith. Sometimes the ABCs of parenting for faith expression are explicitly addressed in adult educational opportunities in the church. Other times this help is not available, and parents are left on their own to figure it out.

This book is written for parents who want the space between birth/adoption and a public affirmation of faith to be an intentional process of Christian identity and formation. In a much earlier time, Horace Bushnell articulated this belief about the purpose of Christian education:

> What is the true idea of Christian education? That the child is to grow up a Christian, and never know [her/him] self as being otherwise. In other words, the aim, effort and expectation should be, not, as is commonly assumed, that the child is to grow up in sin, to be converted after [she/he] comes to a mature age; but that [she/he] is to open on the world as one that is spiritually renewed, not remembering the time when [she/he] went through a technical experience, but seeming rather to have loved what is good from [her/his] earliest year.[3]

The persons most responsible for this kind of Christian education are parents, not church professionals. In this book I am using a very inclusive understanding of family. In today's world, families look very different than they did twenty-five years ago. Parents may be a mother and a father, a single parent, two partners of the same sex, or other family members such as grandparents. Children in a family may be biological and/or adopted. And families may be blended because of divorce or family circumstances.

The excitement, hope, and love that await the birth or adoption of a child sustain a parent through the dailyness of caring for that child. So too, faith, trust, hope, and love become the essential components of parental commitment to the Christian education of a child. Participating in the unfolding of a child's life of faith is truly a gift of God.

However a family is configured, the commitment of faithful adults to making their home a place for faith is essential. Making a home for faith for yourself and your child requires intention and a willingness to live in the in-betweenness of knowing and not knowing, yet trusting in God's presence.

This book is also intended for use in discussion groups in the church. Short-term learning opportunities for parents on Sunday morning or midweek or coffee conversations at a parents' day out are settings where this book might be read and discussed. Another setting for conversation is with parents of preschool and early elementary children, whose children have been baptized or dedicated in worship. Questions at the end of the chapters are designed to be used either by individuals or by groups.

What does God require of us? Nothing more than and everything included in doing justice, loving kindness, and walking humbly with God. By doing these things, we make a home for faith in our lives.

Acknowledgments

And finally some words of thanks. There are four congregations of which I feel a part and which both nurture and challenge my growth in the life of the Christian faith. They all share a commitment to welcoming all of God's people in worship; nurturing children, young people, and adults in varieties of settings for religious education; and offering and encouraging ways of participating in ministries of justice, shalom, and love in their communities and in the world. To the people, pastors, and teachers of Second Presbyterian Church in Nashville, Fourth Presbyterian Church and Lincoln Park Presbyterian Church in Chicago, and Immanuel Presbyterian Church in Milwaukee, I give my thanks.

This book could not have been written without the conversations about children, faith, and life that I have with my sister, Cathy Caldwell Hoop. Her voice is very present in this book through the stories she has shared with me. I am grateful to Cathy and to my friends who have patiently listened to the emerging thoughts and initial ideas that have taken form in this book. Thank you!

1

A HALO, A STAR, AND A BATHROBE: MAKING A HOME FOR FAITH

It was a simple request. We were going home from the Christmas Eve worship service, and two of my nephews were riding with me. From the backseat came four-year-old Christopher's request: "Could we do the nativity when we get home, Lib?" "Sure," I said, curiously wondering what he had in mind.

It took us a while to get together after we reached home, but an executive decision had apparently been made, and the preparations began. Christopher had already changed out of his church clothes into his new bathrobe, and he announced that he would be a shepherd and a wise man. Russell, who was six, said he wanted to be the angel Gabriel. Josh, who was eight, made no request for a part in the nativity. Russell took over as director and said that Mommy and Daddy would be Mary and Joseph, and then he turned to me and said, "And, Lib, you can be a wise man—no, you can be a wise woman."

In about ten minutes we were ready. Some leftover tissue on the table became wings for the angel, and when we moved into the room that was designated as Nazareth, I looked up and saw Josh walking in carrying a very large stick with a yellow tissue-paper star taped to the end. He had obviously chosen the role of props and technical director. I read from Luke, and the angel repeated the words after me.

1

We traveled a great distance to Bethlehem, up the stairs to their bedroom. Josh climbed onto the top bunk, where he sat holding his stick with the star on it over the railing of the bed, and with his other hand he shone a flashlight on the star. Obviously, the shepherds needed the light of the star to guide them. Christopher began to wildly move his arms, a motion I couldn't quite figure out. He was surrounded by a group of stuffed dinosaurs that had been recruited for the evening to be sheep, and Christopher was herding them, as any good shepherd knows to do.

We finally went to the stable. Russell realized that the part of the baby Jesus had not been assigned, so he quickly volunteered. My sister took the halo (a beloved memory from three Christmases past) and put it on baby Jesus' head. The wise man and wise woman, accompanied by the large brown arthritic wise dog, entered carrying their gifts of gold, frankincense, and myrrh, and we all sang "Away in a Manger."

Recall a moment in your life or the life of your family when God's presence was experienced. Remember a time when a connection was made for you between God's Word and your life. This kind of connection is made explicit in Deuteronomy 6:4–9:

> Hear, O Israel: God is our God, God alone. You shall love your God with all your heart, and with all your soul, and with all your might. Keep these words that I am commanding you today in your heart. Recite them to your children and talk about them when you are at home and when you are away, when you lie down and when you rise. Bind them as a sign on your hand, fix them as an emblem on your forehead, and write them on the doorposts of your house and on your gates.

In his commentary on Deuteronomy, Patrick D. Miller notes that chapters 5–11 form the centerpiece of the book because "these are the most important words for those who would cross the border to live as God's people in the place and in the way that God has set for them."[1]

The Shema, or the Great Commandment, as it is called, is a pivotal piece for the rest of Deuteronomy both because of its location, immediately after the Ten Commandments, and because of its placement as a bridge between the Ten Commandments and the explanation of the statutes and ordinances that follow in chapters 12–26. This statement of faith identifies the relationship between God and God's people and names for the people their identity as God's own. Interestingly, it begins with a claim, not a demand: "Hear, O Israel: God is our God, God alone."

The argument of the passage is that if you accept this claim, then the behavior that is expected represents a unity of thinking, believing, and acting: "You shall love your God with all your heart, and with all your soul, and with all your might" or strength—meaning your substance, your wealth, and your property. Lest we think that faithfulness to God is a matter only of intellectual and spiritual assent, we read: keep these words in your heart—make them a part of your very being. Teach them to your children, and remember them wherever you are. Keep them as a sign on your hand and your forehead, and write them on the doorposts of your house. This commandment requires both inward affirmation and visible external practices.

Spending time with a Jewish friend and her family has given me opportunities to participate in rituals of faith that have formed Jews from the very time when these words of Deuteronomy were written. For Reform Jews, the Sabbath begins with a celebration and meal at home and then moves to the synagogue for Friday evening services. "The Shabbat celebration reminds Jewish families to sanctify time and to be aware of God's presence in their lives as they say the blessings, light the candles, drink from the kiddish cup and share the challah."[2]

I like the movement of faith from home to congregation. It represents an integration of faith and life that is essential if church members are committed to being faithful, practicing Christians rather than merely cultural Christians. Facing the prospect of truly being a minority in this culture, we have the opportunity to learn from those who have always been a minority about how to make a home for faith.

JOURNEYS AND HOMES

Growing in faith has been understood in several ways.[3] One metaphor uses natural imagery such as a plant to describe this evolvement. A seed that is nurtured with soil, water, and light grows into a plant. The changes that enable a seedling's growth to the maturity of a plant or tree follow a natural and sequential process.[4]

Another very popular metaphor used to describe the life of the Christian faith is that of a journey or pilgrimage. Like the image of the seed, a journey implies a beginning and an end. But the difference between the two is that "growth and transformation are not so much the development of an internal structure through an expected sequence as they are the results of events and interactions that take place between persons and their environments."[5]

A life begins and a series of events occurs that form a person in faith. For many Christian families, infant baptism or dedication is an important marker in the beginning of a journey of faith that lasts until death when a person's baptism is complete. For C. Ellis Nelson, the most essential interaction that enables growth in the life of faith is an individual's participation in a congregation or community of faith: "My thesis is that faith is communicated by a community of believers and that the meaning of faith is developed by its members out of their history, by their interaction with each other, and in relationship to the events that take place in their lives."[6] Many contemporary religious educators agree with Nelson that it is within the faith community that a person's journey in faith is both supported and challenged and so grows and evolves over time.[7]

A third metaphor describes the nature and the process of growing in faith. Homemaking or making a home for faith is a concept that resonates with the intent of Deuteronomy 6:4–9. I use it not so much in opposition to the images of natural growth or journeys in faith but as an addition. This concept has become apparent from observation and from reflection on reading. Rather than conceiving of a life of faith in terms of a growing seed or a road, consider a home with windows and light, a door, a room. This home is unique to each person, and so some "homes for faith" can be found in tree houses or tents, apartments or mansions, cabins in the woods or balconies with window boxes near the train tracks. Making a home for faith is concerned with the intentionality of being aware of God and God's presence wherever you are.

Think about people who are never "at home" with their faith. There are several kinds of homeless Christians. Have you ever met people who are always searching for answers? Their faith does not bring them comfort or assurance; it brings only anguish, uncertainty, or dissatisfaction. In a recent book for children of all ages, *God in Between,* Sandy Eisenberg Sasso described people who lived in a town with no roads or windows. With no way to look out or beyond their village, they wondered about the existence of God. And so they sent out "The Ones Who Could See Out Windows," hoping they would find evidence of God. When they came back without finding God, the people in the town decided there was no God. After their return, "The Ones Who Could See Out Windows" began helping the people build roads to connect their houses, and windows so they could see outside their homes. In this activity, they came to know that God was "in the between. In between us."[8] I believe that some people, like those in the story that Sasso tells, are so busy going on a pilgrimage looking for God that they fail to recognize God's daily presence in their lives.

Other people believe that faith is imported to them from "theological experts." "Tell me what to believe" is their request. They can't or won't trust what they have learned or what they have experienced in life. Their "vocabulary of faith" to name and reflect on their knowledge and experiences is woefully inadequate.[9] The faith they affirm in worship each Sunday somehow is not integrated with their lives. Afraid of making a theological or biblical faux pas, they do little for themselves, failing to trust even the simplest faith affirmations.

Reading the Bible, which can open a person to the depths of the mysteries of God and faith, is a scary thought to those who believe that experts should tell them how to read and what to think. In his book *God's Mailbox: More Stories about Stories in the Bible,* Marc Gellman has a word for people like this: "READ THE BIBLE RIGHT AWAY! If you do, something great will happen. You will find hope for when your hope has died. You will find joy for when you are sad. You will find words that teach you the right way to live when you are not doing the right thing."[10]

Among a third group are people who rely on one hour of worship a week to provide what they need for growing in the life of the Christian faith. Faith is more a cultural identity than a religious one. When faced with a life crisis or an ethical decision, they are homeless.

The theologian and educator Nelle Morton once said she had come to realize that "home was not a place. Home is a movement, a quality of relationship, a state where people seek to be 'their own' and increasingly responsible for their world."[11] For those for whom the Christian life is more an activity of public participation or familial expectation than personal identity, faith is segmented, assigned to a place unrelated to the rest of life and vocation.

The tension present in the metaphor "making a home for faith" is one of affirming a life lived in the assurance of the presence of God while acknowledging the difficult challenge to live faithfully in the world in response to our baptism. In an article he wrote many years ago, Walter Brueggemann remarked that "confirmation is joining a crunch. . . . The life of Christian faith is a life of profound bother. It is centered in the awareness that there is an incongruity between what is and what God has intended."[12] Those who are committed to making a home for faith affirm that living a "bothered life" is of importance and a priority for them.

Making a home for faith includes both affirmation and action. As Sharon Parks has said, "We grow and become both by letting go and holding on, leaving and staying, journeying and abiding. A good life is a balance of home and pilgrimage."[13] The commitment to living with this balance is surely the calling of all who would call themselves faithful.

TABLES, STORIES, AND WINDOWS

Three household images illustrate the tasks involved in making a home for faith. They have implications for families and for congregations as they conceptualize and practice religious education that leads to faithful knowing, being, and doing.

The first image is a table. In his chapter "Christian Education in a Pluralistic Culture" in the book *Rethinking Christian Education,* Martin Marty says that "many participants in Christian education are refugees, exiles or rebels."[14] He believes that a major task for those of us in Christian education is to help people make sense of the world—but the place setting on the table is missing, so to speak.

In other words many of those who claim to be Christian do not know enough of the biblical story or the teachings of the church of which they are a part. They are hampered in their ability to name their faith and live its practices in an increasingly pluralistic culture.

Marty suggests that another reality of Christians is that "many who are in Christian education have had little experience of other spiritual menus."[15] Their faith becomes a shelter or carapace to protect them from the world and all of its diversity. Others refuse responsibility for learning and leading with the faith community and turn over the work of setting the table of faith to the professionals. After all, the ministers and religious educators are hired to do that, aren't they? Prepared take-out meals can now be applied to faith and learning about God. It can all be done in one hour on Sunday morning!

It is essential that faith communities support people in the articulation of their belief systems. For Christians to believe that they are living in a predominantly Christian culture is unrealistic. The impact of the Christian faith on our culture continues to diminish as membership in mainline denominations declines and people search for meaning in their lives in a world that is increasingly complex, violent, and divided between the very rich and the very poor.

Children grow up biblically illiterate in homes where Bibles abound but are rarely opened. We have become a generation incapable of passing on the stories of our faith. The face of our faith has become extremely impoverished. Instead of being rich banquets, feasts of faith and community, our tables of faith become barren with barely enough bread and water to satisfy, and we try to sustain ourselves on this meager diet.

It is imperative that congregations support and educate adults in ways that will enable them to set tables of faith in their homes, tables of faith that move with them to communities of faith who gather at another table to share in the feast of God. Parents become able to read a biblical story with their children, listen to their questions, and struggle with answers together. Setting a table of faith in our homes means we have time for rituals, for practices that form us in our faith and sustain us as we leave home to journey into the world. Journeys or pilgrimages in faith require faithful homemaking and table setting.

Keep these words that I am commanding you today in your heart.

A second image is that of stories. I believe that Marty is right about refugees, exiles, and rebels. Our churches are full of people who have run from one faith tradition to find another. Young adults stand outside the windows, exiled at confirmation, wondering if there is a place for them. Rebels of faith of all ages, those who yearn for deep conversations and hard dialogue about faith, search for a satisfying menu or opportunities to think, discuss, reflect on Scripture and its meaning for their lives—something more than what is offered in a typical program of adolescent or adult religious education.

I think the Christmas we "did the nativity" will be a story that will be retold in our family for many years to come. In telling a story, we remember who we are, and we connect it to an event, a moment in time, a place, and the experience of it all. And implicitly and sometimes explicitly, we discuss its meaning and its implication for the present and the future.

Two books contribute to helping people of faith remember and retell their stories. In *Practicing Our Faith: A Way of Life for a Searching People,* the authors explore twelve historic Christian practices, which are defined as "things Christian people do together over time in response to and in light of God's active presence for the life of the world."[16] The practices include honoring the body, offering hospitality, applying household economics, saying yes and saying no, keeping sabbath, expressing testimony, having discernment, shaping communities, being forgiving, healing, dying well, and singing our lives. "Entering more deeply into a Christian practice, we do not just learn the practice. When practices are faithful, they teach us surprising things about God, our neighbors and the world."[17]

In *Common Fire: Lives of Commitment in a Complex World,* the authors studied the lives and told the stories of more than one hundred people who they believe live and work on behalf of the common good, people who possess a shared sense of participation and responsibility in the world. The authors described the people they interviewed in this way: "Over the years their hearts' deep gladness became so integrated with the world's deep hunger that they found a home in that 'sweet spot' where everything connects and were finally unable to turn away from its claim on them. They could not 'just say no.'"[18]

When read together, these books have the potential for enabling reflection on our stories of practices and our commitments to the common good—the unity of being and doing at the heart of the Shema, "you shall love your God with all your heart, and with all your soul, and with all your might." Making a home for faith requires intention, space, and time. Exiles, rebels, and refugees can become storytellers at home with a faith that can nurture and sustain them for a life lived in commitment in the world. Sharon Daloz Parks, one of the authors of *Common Fire*, noted in an earlier article: "Home-making . . . is a connective, creative act of the human imagination and a primary activity of the Spirit. It is the creation of forms and patterns which cultivate and shelter life itself. Homemaking and homesteading are activities which build a space where souls can thrive and dream—secure, protected, related, nourished and whole."[19]

Making a home for faith is equally important in a community of faith. Creating a space for learning where important issues of faith and life can be discussed must be a commitment of both congregations and the individual adult learners who are part of the faith community. In *Caretakers of Our Common House*, Carol Lakey Hess describes the tension between "hard dialogue and deep connections," which takes place in "conversational education." Hess says that "the background for hard dialogue in communities of faith is our deep connection in God."[20]

"Homelessness of faith" can be replaced by faces of faith when adults and congregations affirm the need for participation in opportunities for learning in the Christian faith. Instruction becomes possible only when the need for learning is acknowledged as a lifelong commitment to tending a household of faith.

> Recite them to your children and talk about them when you are at home and when you are away, when you lie down and when you rise.

The third image is that of windows. In one of her earlier novels, *A Severed Wasp*, Madeleine L'Engle describes Felix, who introduces himself as a window cleaner. His conversation partner knew he was a violinist and queried, "A window cleaner and a violinist?" "No *and*," [he replied.] "Music is my window cleaning. . . . All our windows have been so fouled with futility and folly that we can't see out. So there have to be window cleaners. Artists, he said, would clean the muddied windows with the purity of their art."[21]

Who or what cleans the windows of your soul? What opportunities have pushed open the window of your thinking and allowed a breath of air to come in and raise questions about yourself, your faith, your place, your commitments, your call, or your vocation? I think that each person of faith is a theologian, and so by nature we are also window cleaners. We stand, convinced and convicted, in our beliefs. We live and we act. We also listen to others, and in listening and being and doing, we help others to remove some of the mud that prevents seeing. We help one another open windows a bit to see from a different perspective.

Dwayne Huebner has spoken of the role that faith plays as a "clearing in our everydayness, a place for acknowledging God. . . . As we begin to construct our human world and our understanding of ourselves in that world, we fail to save clearings for remembering and praising God and for seeking God's presence. In building our human world and our understanding we, in effect, construct idols that detract us from memory, praise and hope."[22]

Cleaning the windows and knowing when to open and close them seem to me to be essential parts of maintaining a home for faith.

> Bind [these words] as a sign on your hand, fix them as an emblem on your forehead, and write them on the doorposts of your house and on your gates.

A psalmist has confessed that the statutes of God "have been my songs in the house of my pilgrimage" (Ps. 119:54 KJV). The New Revised Standard Version translates "house of my pilgrimage" as "wherever I make my home."

> In homemaking, the congregation works to help its people learn the songs and stories of God so that this presence is with them wherever they make their home. Moreover, the congregation makes a commitment to send people out, blessed with the waters of baptism and nourished at the table of Jesus Christ. They go forth with a story, faith and an expectation for responsible Christian living. These are the tangible yet intangible gifts which accompany them in the houses of their pilgrimage in the world.[23]

After I left Nashville at Christmas that year, Christopher told his mother that we had left out two parts of the nativity. He did not say which ones, but I'm sure he knows. He also said that the next year he wanted to be the angel Gabriel and the baby Jesus.

A table of faith was set, a story was told, and a window for me that had been clouded over with pressures of work and the stress of travel and holiday preparations was washed clean. The words of Moses are truly timeless. Surely in the borders we cross each day as we attempt to live as God's people, we, too, need to remember these "most important words."

> Hear, O Israel: God is our God, God alone. You shall love your God with all your heart, and with all your soul, and with all your might.

QUESTIONS FOR REFLECTION AND DISCUSSION

1. How would you describe the evolvement of your life of faith? What images best illustrate your experiences?
2. In what ways was your faith nurtured or not nurtured in your home when you were a child or youth? What practices were a priority in enabling your growth in the life of the Christian faith?
3. What faith questions do you remember as being important to you when you were a child or youth? Who was there to listen or respond to these questions?
4. When it comes to thinking about faith, of what are you most confident? Least confident? Which questions of faith would you most like to ask your pastor?
5. What faith question has your child asked recently? How did you respond?

PARENTING FOR FAITH EXPRESSION

Intentional Christian nurture is necessary
because our culture shapes children for a world shorn of
God . . . religious education must begin at home and
at an early age.[1]

The Hebrew Scriptures (Old Testament) tell the story of God's covenant with God's people. God sent priests, judges, kings and queens, and prophets to tell of God's Word. First Kings tells the story of the Israelites after King David and a prophet named Elijah who was sent by God with a message for King Ahab. You can read this story beginning in First Kings 16.

Elijah was somewhat of a reluctant prophet, like others we meet in the biblical story. After delivering his message to King Ahab, Elijah left town, fearing for his life. He begged God to let him die. In the midst of Elijah's terror and anxiety for his life and future, God appeared to him twice, first in the form of an angel who told him to "get up and eat, otherwise the journey will be too much for you" (1 Kings 19:7). Elijah did what the angel said and regained his strength and traveled to Horeb, known as the mount of God. God found him there and asked what he was doing in the cave. Elijah confessed his commitment to God as well as the fear for his life.

God told Elijah to go out and stand on the mountain. There was a great wind, but God was not in the wind. Then there was an earthquake, but God was not in the earthquake. After the earthquake, there was a fire, but God was not in the fire. "And after the fire a sound of sheer silence. When Elijah heard it, he wrapped his face in his mantle and went out and stood at the entrance of the cave" (1 Kings 19:12–13).

A child has come into your life by birth or adoption. You wonder about many things—who this child is, who this child will become, what your role as a parent of this child will be. You ask, Will I be good enough? Do I know enough? What will the journey with this child look like?

God came to Elijah in the form of bread that would sustain his life as he sought to escape those who wanted to end it. God also came to Elijah in the "sound of sheer silence." Notice the next phrase, "when Elijah heard it." God told Elijah to step out on the mountain because God was about to pass by. And God did! Elijah did not see God, but Elijah heard God.

This chapter seeks to examine the role of parents as primary faith educators. Some might say, "Wait a minute. That's why our family goes to church school and joins in the worship service. The professionals know what they are doing in this matter. I don't." The reality is, a parent or parents have many more opportunities for educating their child in the life of the Christian faith than church school teachers do in one hour, once a week.

The title for this chapter, "Parenting for Faith Expression," has been chosen to communicate the expectation and hope for the way adults can grow into their role as primary faith educators with their child or children. The role assumes a certain amount of knowledge, a commitment to faithful Christian living in the world, and most important, a way of being in the presence of God. Like Elijah, we can affirm that God will provide bread for this journey and that in moments of uncertainty or doubt, God is there even in the "sound of sheer silence."

PARENTS AS FAITH EDUCATORS—BEING, KNOWING, AND DOING

Preparation to live with a face of faith in the world requires that adult Christians make intentional commitments to nurturing their faith—both individually and communally. Establishing regular patterns of spiritual formation, habits of mind and heart, have the power to feed hungry souls and form a face of faith that can meet the world with all of its demands and challenges.[2]

A religious educator has identified three kinds of parents of children in the church school. First are the parents who believe their days are "full enough and are perfectly willing to leave the education of their children to others, not recognizing their own inevitable part in that education."[3] Second are the "harassed parents," whose time and energy are focused on providing the basics of food, shelter, and clothing for their children. Though possessing the best of intentions to be good parents, they have no time left over to "learn to be intelligent educators."[4] Third are the parents who joyously pursue any opportunity to be involved in the Christian life of their children and programs of Christian education in their church.

Writing about these three kinds of parents in 1929, Hulda Niebuhr was concerned with parental education and believed it should be a major priority for the church. Helping parents claim their identity as faith educators is also the concern of a more recent educator, Dwayne Huebner, who describes the life of faith of a parent as being cluttered or one that makes space and time for a clearing for God.

> The infant, in growing with a cluttered adult and without the necessary clearings for remembering, thinking, and seeking God, constructs or takes on idols, not clearings of faith. The structures of receptivity—of hearing, seeing, feeling—are cluttered and faithless, because the consciousness of the adult is cluttered and faithless. So also the structures of action—of reaching out and doing, of relating to others. And finally, so are the structures of thinking and symbolizing.[5]

While Niebuhr is concerned with a parent's active involvement in the formation of her or his child in the Christian faith, Huebner is concerned with the faith of the parent. Another theologian, Mark Searle, makes clear the connection between being in faith and living in faith. In speaking of the promises made by parents at the baptism of children, Searle believes this is more than a vow to teach them what they know.

> Instead, they commit themselves anew to learning the story by living it, and it is chiefly by the parents living the Christian story that their children will come to pick it up and to develop the skills necessary to be faithful to it. The story and the skills are only partially conveyed in explicit lessons. Christianity, it has been said, is more caught than taught, and the model for learning it is closer to that of an apprenticeship than that of a classroom.[6]

For Searle, knowledge is more than the ability to tell the story of Miriam saving the life of her brother, Moses, or of Mary and Martha preparing to welcome Jesus to their home. Knowledge is intimately connected with being faithful and having that evidenced in daily living.

In an introduction to one of his books, Marc Gellman describes what is required of one who would write about stories in the Bible. Such a person has to love the Bible, love God, and love people.[7] In describing the Bible, he says it "is kind of like a pair of glasses through which I look at the world. I see our stories in its stories. I see all of us in all of them, and most of all I see God there and I see God here."[8]

I agree with Niebuhr, Searle, and Huebner in their emphasis on the intentionality required of faithful parents in being faithful and in living faithfully in the world. I also want to affirm the importance of the activity of knowing. To make use of the glasses that Gellman describes, one has to take them out of the case. A frame for being and doing in the world is enabled by the ability to be at home with the biblical story. Making a clearing for God and serving as a role model for a young apprentice in faith assume knowledge, understanding, and a wrestling with the biblical story in order to understand God's Word to us then, now, and in the future we cannot see or know.

CLEARING OUT SOME ROOM

> I will have nothing to do with a God who cares only occasionally. I need a God who is with us always, everywhere, in the deepest depths as well as the highest heights.

It is when things go wrong, when the good things do not happen, when our prayers seem to have been lost, that God is most present. We do not need the sheltering wings when things go smoothly. We are closest to God in the darkness, stumbling along blindly. . . .

We need to say "thank you" whenever possible, even if we are not able to reconcile the human creature's will with the Maker's working out of the pattern. Thanks and praise are, I believe, some of the threads with which the pattern is woven.[9]

I come from a long line of "closet stuffers." This awareness was confirmed when my family gathered to clean out the apartment of my grandmother who died at age 102 in 1998. We laughed and cried, and we told stories recalled by the stuff we unloaded from her closets. I think my sister and mother and I all returned home vowing to immediately clean the clutter out of our closets so no one would have to face that task for us. But then, we got busy after we returned to our homes, and of course, the closet cleaning, which has never been a priority, fell to the bottom of the list of household chores.

Making a home for faith in our lives requires that we tackle the mess—clean the closets, so to speak, of some things that get in the way of good intentions. We must examine the stuff that prevents us from making space for reflection, contemplation, and engagement with the life of the Christian faith. I like Huebner's image of "a clearing in the midst of the busy-ness of life, in the jungle of our doings, concerns and worries."[10] In speaking of faith, Huebner believes that such a place represents not emptiness but a "clearing for God's presence, the Spirit. Jesus instructs those of little faith to 'Seek first God's kingdom and God's righteousness.' The image is of a clearing in the midst of our everydayness wherein God is sought, waited for, acknowledged, depended upon. Faith is an awareness of God's presence. God is easily forgotten during the busy-ness of the everydayness. Faith is remembering God."[11]

For some, like Madeleine L'Engle, prayer is a way of remembering God. Conversation with God, however brief, at the beginning or closing of the day sustains a parent whose day provides few moments of solitude or silence. For parents who have made a commitment to teach in the church school, reading curricular materials and biblical references and thinking about teaching are excellent ways of making a "clearing for God's presence." But additional practices of faith help remove the clutter.

One way to organize the closet, to clear space for remembering God, is to consider the variety of practices and disciplines of the Christian faith. It has been said that growing in the life of the Christian faith involves a "lifelong continuing process of encountering into the inexhaustible richness of the mystery of God and of God's love, ever more deeply and profoundly."[12] This process requires intention and practice, and is supported by participation in communities of faith. "We come to recognize and live in the Spirit as we participate more and more broadly and deeply in communities that know the nature of their situation, acknowledge it, express it, and live their lives in light of it."[13]

Review this list of Christian practices that have been identified as consistent with the Reformed tradition. Which ones are a part of your life of faith? Are there any surprises on the list, any that make you say, "Aha—I hadn't thought of that one"?

Worshiping

Telling the Christian story

Interpreting Scripture

Praying

Confessing sin and reconciling

Encouraging others

Being in service and witnessing

Suffering with neighbors

Providing hospitality and care

Listening

Struggling to understand the context of life

Criticizing and resisting the powers of evil

Working together to create social structures that sustain life in accord with God's will[14]

If we return to the formative activities of being, knowing, and doing described earlier, it is possible to see in what ways these practices are illustrative.

- Being—worshiping, listening, praying, struggling to understand the context of life, suffering with neighbors

- Knowing—telling the Christian story, interpreting Scripture, confessing sin and reconciling

- Doing—encouraging others, providing hospitality and care, being in service and witnessing, criticizing and resisting the powers of evil, working together to create social structures that sustain life in accord with God's will

The activity of being in faith includes the practices listed but does not exclude others such as reading the Bible and reflecting on its historical context and present meanings. Considering the practices from this angle of vision enables us to recognize both the simplicity and the complexity expected of one who seeks to make a home for faith in his or her life.

Upon observing the numbers of people who were in attendance at a Christmas Eve service, many who were not regular attendees, someone asked the pastor why they came. The minister responded, "It is the only story they know."[15] Faithful practices including participation in the life of a congregation enable adults, children, and young people to know more than one story.

MORE THAN TABLE BLESSINGS

> The most persuasive moral teaching we adults do is by example: the witness of our lives, our ways of being with others and speaking to them and getting on with them— all of that taken in slowly, cumulatively, by our sons and daughters, our students . . . in the long run of a child's life, the unself-conscious moments that are what we think of simply as the unfolding events of the day and the week turn out to be the really powerful and persuasive times, morally.[16]

If you asked adults what is involved in homemaking, you would probably hear a variety of answers. Whether the task is fixing a leaking roof or preparing a nutritious meal, most would agree that a lot of time, energy, and commitment is involved in making a home. In the last few years of talking with parents about nurturing their children's faith, I have begun to compile a list of their children's questions that they really hope someone can answer. They go like this:

Why is there evil?

Why does God let terrible things happen?

Where is heaven? Is my dog there?

Why isn't God doing the same miracles today as in Jesus' time? Such as talking directly to us? I know God is doing miracles in a different way today, not the direct approach. I would like it done both ways.

I frame the questions about authority, knowledge, and responsibility of parents in making themselves at home with faith by asking them these questions: If you can't get Wishbone home, what do you do? (Wishbone is a dog in a computer program for children, and the task involves getting Wishbone home from his world travels.) If you can't solve a math problem, what do you do? If you've forgotten what personification is and how to write a sentence using one, how do you help your child with her homework assignment?

A colleague began a workshop for parents on faith and their children by asking these questions: Which would you rather explain to your child: How babies are born, or why are violence and killing so much a part of the biblical stories in the Hebrew Scriptures? How the motor in your car works, or what Easter means? The responses from the parents were fairly equally split between the answers.[17]

Being comfortable with a child's wonderings and questions requires that an adult be at home with his or her own faith. After listening to the kinds of children's questions that parents want an "expert" to answer, I have become convinced of the importance of giving adults something more than immediate answers to specific questions. Helping parents name and claim their own faith tradition and theological affirmations seems to be a more useful life skill than memorizing a list of answers to specific questions. It is not enough for a parent to offer a table blessing at meals. Parenting for faith expression assumes a commitment to and a priority for growing in the life of the Christian faith.

One way to think about the movement and changes involved as one is nurtured in a life of faith is to engage in writing and reflecting on affirmations of faith. In many Christian faith traditions, a statement of faith is included in the service of worship. Usually following the sermon, the saying together of the Apostles' Creed or the Nicene Creed or a contemporary statement of faith involves the congregation in publicly affirming, "Here I stand; this is what I believe."

A faith statement is a theological document. It attempts to make explicit a person's understanding of and connections with basic tenets of the Christian faith. There are two groups of people for whom the writing and sharing of faith statements are often required. Students graduating from seminaries or theological schools and preparing for their ordination as ministers of Word and Sacrament are asked to write a statement of faith. It gives them a chance to articulate their faith, integrating in a few pages, knowledge, experience, and reflection on the Christian faith and the life of the Christian in the church and the world.

Confirmands, twelve- to eighteen-year-olds preparing to make their public statement of faith, are a second group for whom the articulation of a faith statement is often expected. Sometimes they are given the option of choosing the form for this faith expression: words, art, music, dance. Many adults have been powerfully affected by hearing young people express their faith convictions. (For examples, see appendix 1.)

On occasions when I have been a part of a congregation hearing the faith statements of young people, I have often wished that the liturgy would include a place for the involvement of the parents of those being confirmed. This idea came from being present at a Shabbat service in a Reform Jewish congregation on the evening before a young person's bat mitzvah. After the young woman read from the Torah, her parents came forward and also read in Hebrew. At this moment of public recognition of years of religious education and preparation of faith, a child and her parents are expected to be able to read the word of God from the Torah.

What if all young people at their confirmation or believer's baptism were accompanied by their parents, who also affirmed their faith? Parents might attend a discussion group to prepare them for their participation with their children. But then the hope is that their whole lives of faith, as well as their role as ones who have made a commitment to parent the children for their own expression of faith, have prepared them for this public moment.

Turn to the faith statement form included in appendix 2. Use it as a way to examine your theological convictions, questions, and areas of mystery and wonder about God.

BEING ON "MANNA ALERT"[18]

There is a liturgical rhythm that moves us from our home table to the communion table. At both tables, we remember family stories, we give thanks for food and nourishment, we claim God's presence, we eat together. In all of these activities we proclaim who we are as Christians and help form the world as God intends it to be. These table activities have the power to form and transform us. Such forming and transforming is essential in our culture.[19]

After they left Egypt and began wandering in the wilderness, following a cloud by day and a pillar of fire by night, the Israelites grew hungry. God heard their cries and promised them, "At twilight you shall eat meat, and in the morning you shall have your fill of bread; then you shall know that I am your God" (Exod. 16:12). When the Israelites awoke the next morning, the ground was covered with what looked like white frost. And they asked, "What is it?" The white flaky stuff was called manna, and it tasted like "wafers made with honey" (Exod. 16:31). The text goes on to say that the Israelites ate manna for forty years "until they came to a habitable land" (Exod. 16:35).

Barbara Brown Taylor suggests that when we start complaining, asking God why God can't send a lovely loaf of warm crusted bread instead of manna, we miss the ordinary things God does every day in our lives. And so she says she is on "manna alert," which involves being attentive to God. If "you are willing to look at everything that comes to you as coming from God, then there will be no end to the manna in your life."[20]

In her book *The Shelter of Each Other: Rebuilding Our Families,* Mary Pipher addresses the concerns of culture's influence on its children and the place and value of family within the culture. She says that she is concerned with "family ecology and family well-being."[21] Her book concludes with six strategies for protecting families, ones that she believes "give the family definition, identity and power."[22] They include protecting family time and making family rituals a priority; identifying places or spots that have meaning for a family; engaging in interests shared by family members such as music, sports, or gardening; honoring individual rites of passage as well as family celebrations; engaging in rituals that connect family members to one another, to extended family, to friends, and to the larger community; and recalling family stories and metaphors that "stand for what the family loves and values."[23]

What is noticeable about this list is what is missing. I believe that faith, life in a faithful family, and participation in a congregation shelter families. Nurturing faith in a child, honoring sabbath, and struggling with theological questions also give families identity and power to make a difference in the culture. Faith shelters families when the members are on "manna alert," open to the mysteries of the presence of God in their lives.

John Westerhoff has identified five guidelines for sharing faith with children from birth through childhood in his book *Bringing Up Children in the Christian Faith*. These guidelines illustrate in simple ways how faith can shelter a family. Westerhoff believes that adults in a family should tell and retell the biblical story together. We should become better storytellers, ones who read the Bible and attempt to understand the variety of writings it contains. "We need to learn to tell the [biblical] story as our story. And the purpose of our learning to do so is always the same: to transform individual and social life so that God's will might be done and God's kingdom might come."[24]

Celebrating faith and lives with family rituals is another way of growing in faith together. Westerhoff believes that rituals honoring celebrations of the family and the church calendar (Advent, Christmas, Epiphany, Lent, Easter, Pentecost, All Saints' Day) enable family members to connect the daily and the holy. Questions to consider in thinking about celebrations include: "What occasions are we going to make special? How will we prepare? What will we do? What part of the story will we remember? What part of our story will we enact? How will we involve children?"[25]

Another guideline is praying together. Praying involves listening and speaking, being aware of God's presence. Prayers of adoration, confession, praise, thanksgiving, and intercession can be practiced by each member of a family. "To share with our children a life in friendship with God is to pray and to learn to pray."[26]

Living our faith with children can be as simple as listening and talking with each other. In the asking of religious questions, Westerhoff believes that what "children are really asking is for us to reveal and share ourselves and our faith, not to provide dogmatic answers. We do not need to answer our children's questions, but we do need to make our faith available to them as a source for their learning and growth."[27]

Performing faithful acts of service and witness together enables a family to make connections between the biblical story and its practice in everyday life. Westerhoff believes that faith requires three things: a way of perceiving, looking at the world as God's realm; a way of relating, "living in the presence and companionship of God";[28] and a way of acting in God's name in the world. Adults who want to share their faith with children can do nothing better than take them along with them to engage in acts of service.

FAITH LIFE OF THE FAMILY

> Whenever a child is presented for baptism, it will be the responsibility of the local community to discern whether this child is certainly called to the life of faith by looking at the faith life of the family.[29]

> Without a Christian calendar functioning in the festive life of a family, the landscape of family celebration will be filled with whatever our cultural calendars have to offer.[30]

Mark Searle's suggestion about calling for a family to critically examine its faith life is worthy of discussion. Perhaps if this idea was taken seriously, it might be easier for parents to stand with their teenager at confirmation or baptism and affirm the faith in which they have their lives and beings. The time in between birth or adoption and a child's naming and claiming his or her faith presents many opportunities for sharing and living the Christian faith.

A reality of life today for many families is the demands on their time. The attempt to balance the requirements of work, home, school, extracurricular activities for children, and participation and leadership in a congregation is a difficult one. Free time has become almost nonexistent for many families. In therapy sessions, Mary Pipher listened to families talk about their lives and determined that what was lacking were the "nourishing activities" that people recall with pleasure: meals, vacations or free time spent together, time outdoors. Pipher has observed that "when families get too busy, the first things that go are their rituals."[31]

Think about the life of your family when you were a child. What family rituals were important to you—reading bedtime stories, taking family bike rides or hikes, putting out the nativity at Christmas, dyeing Easter eggs together? Which ones have you continued in your own family?

A family moves into a new home and wants to have some kind of ritual or blessing to begin life in a new place. In planning for the celebration of the eight nights of Hanukkah and the tradition of giving a small gift to a child, a Jewish parent is concerned about how much her children already have. They begin a new ritual of giving away a toy that they are no longer playing with.

A long-awaited child has been born or adopted by a parent or parents. In addition to having birthday cakes and candles, they want to remember this day in a special way. They create a photo album of the child's first pictures in their new family. And on the day of birth or adoption, a ritual of bringing out the album and retelling the story continues year after year.

Tom Driver describes ritual as a "deep human longing" and believes it is essential to rethink ritual in connection with religious life.[32] I agree with Pipher and Driver about the importance and need for ritual in our lives. I also believe that making space for rituals contributes to the faith life of a family. It enables connections to be made with the rituals of worship and the sacraments in the life of a faith community.

In his cross-cultural study of ritual and its place in human life, Driver has identified two definitions for the purpose and function of ritual in our lives. Rituals are pathways, and ritualizing is the "making of these paths for behavior to follow."[33] Rituals are also performance and as such are more than behavior. In this sense rituals work to enable "acting in the world."[34] As such they can be both confessional and ethical. "An ethical act is one that is willing to be seen."[35]

In the second half of his book, Driver identifies three benefits that rituals give to a community. First, they establish order in the sense of marking time and space and are factitive; they make things happen.[36] Second, rituals bring people together in community, and in this shared space there is the possibility for spontaneity, play, expressions of affection, and a sense of unity in being together. Third, rituals have the potential for transformation.

Driver's thinking about the need for ritual in our lives helps to name the simple things that families do to contribute to a life of faith. What if we considered David Batchelder's suggestion about a Christian calendar that would function in the life of a family? Such a calendar might look like the one presented here.

Use the calendar as a guide for reflecting on the rituals of your family life and the ways they strengthen and support the faith life of your family. A few suggestions are given to get you started, and more ideas are described in chapter 5. Use any blank space in the calendar to fill in your thoughts.

As you consider your present family rituals and new ones you might like to add, keep in mind Westerhoff's five criteria for sharing faith with children: telling stories, celebrating, praying, living our faith, and performing faithful acts of service and witness. Recall Driver's two definitions, and use them to examine family rituals. In participating in these rituals, what pathways of faith are being laid by our family? What actions in the world are enabled by this ritual?

LIVING BREAD AND LIVING WATER

When Jesus was teaching his disciples, a large crowd began to gather. As Jesus looked over the crowd, he wondered aloud with the disciples about how they were going to be fed. If they had been polled, the disciples would have voted to send the people home to find their own food and lodging, since there did not appear to be a bounty of food available in the deserted place in which they were meeting. Jesus had another idea and told the disciples, "You give them something to eat" (Luke 9:13). His instruction must have really caught them by surprise since the only food they had noticed in the crowd was the lunch of a boy who had brought five loaves and two fish with him.

And you know the rest of this story, which is told by all four Gospel writers. Jesus took the bread and blessed it, and everyone received food: "All ate and were filled" (Luke 9:17).

On another occasion, Jesus was traveling through Samaria. He was tired and thirsty, so he sat down by Jacob's well. When he saw

Month	Seasonal Emphasis (Liturgical and Cultural)	Family Activity
January	Epiphany—twelfth night of Christmas	Invite friends over to celebrate the visit of the Magi to the Christchild. Recall the visit of the Magi and imagine what Gifts we could give to the Christchild.
	Kwanzaa	
	Martin Luther King's Birthday	Use this month to read stories of modern-day prophets who have worked to make God's peace and justice a reality for all. Tell stories of Dorothy Day, Mary McLeod Bethune, Rosa Parks, Ruby Bridges.
February	Valentine's Day	Make valentines together; deliver some to neighbors and disabled or elderly persons in the church who live alone.
	Ash Wednesday— beginning of Lent	
March	Lent	
April	Holy Week Easter	
May	May Day/Earth Week Pentecost	
June		
July		
August		
September		
October	Worldwide Communion Sunday	
	Halloween	
	All Saint's Day	
November	Thanksgiving	
	Beginning of Advent	Table blessings—sing a verse of a hymn learned in church school, choir, or worship during Advent.
December	Advent Christmas	

a Samaritan woman come to the well, he asked her for a drink. She let Jesus know that she was astonished by his request since Jews and Samaritans did not share anything. Jesus said, "If you knew the gift of God, and who it is that is saying to you, 'Give me a drink,' you would have asked him, and he would have given you living water" (John 4:10). She was intrigued and wanted to know the source of this "living water." Jesus explained that those who drink "living water" that he gives, they will never be thirsty again. And the woman said, "Give me this water, so that I may never be thirsty or have to keep coming here to draw water" (John 4:15). The story continues, revealing Jesus' knowledge of the woman's background. It concludes with Jesus' revelation of himself and the woman's affirmation of faith.

After Jesus Christ's death and resurrection, he was walking on the road to Emmaus and met two of his disciples who engaged in conversation with him but did not know who he was. At the meal that evening, in the breaking of the bread, "their eyes were opened, and they recognized him" (Luke 24:31).

Bread and water, the basic elements of a daily diet, become something more in these stories. The people in the stories are always caught by surprise, and we are left to wonder, What did they hear, what did they see, what did they understand about bread that satisfies hunger both physical and spiritual? Did they appreciate the difference between water that quenches immediate thirst and living water? And then we insert ourselves in the story: When do we acknowledge our own hunger and thirst for something more?

World Communion Sunday is one of my favorite liturgical celebrations in the church. On the first Sunday in October, Christians all over the world affirm that there is one table of Jesus Christ, and on that day, we recognize the diversity in our unity in the Christian faith. And so the table is filled with living bread—pita bread, rice cakes, tortillas, sliced white bread, bread made with herbs from a garden, whole-grain bread from midwestern wheat fields. And we celebrate the unity of Christians in Korea, South America, Africa, the Middle East, and Europe who acknowledge one God, who is Creator, Redeemer, and Sustainer. World Communion Sunday also helps us remember the variety of families around the table: single-parent families, two-parent families, partners raising an adopted child, and extended families of friends who love and nurture children in the life of the Christian faith.

My hope is that parenting for faith expression will help adults seek the living water and living bread that sustain a life of faith. Making a clearing for God can ensure that the one story of Jesus' birth, life, death, and resurrection can empower us for lives of faith lived in families, within congregations, and throughout the world.

QUESTIONS FOR REFLECTION AND DISCUSSION

1. Describe the clearing for God in your life.
2. What idols prevent your engaging in memory, praise, and hope in God?
3. When you consider the role of a parent as faith educator and the activities of knowing, being, and doing, where is your strength/weakness?
4. Which practices of faith are ones you find meaningful? Which are ones you have not tried but would like to consider?
5. What biblical stories or passages have had the most impact on your life of faith?
6. What biblical stories would you like to know more about?
7. Read and discuss some historic and contemporary statements of faith, for example: Apostles' Creed, Nicene Creed, or a contemporary creedal statement of your denomination or congregation. What in this creed can you affirm? Where do you have questions or concerns? Compare any of these creeds with your personal statement of faith. Where are they alike or different?
8. In what ways has your faith statement evolved since you were a teenager?
9. Look at the headings and the quotes that begin each section of this chapter. What themes or images do you want to remember?
10. After reading John Westerhoff's five guidelines for sharing faith with children, which ones are a part of your family? Tell a story about one of them.
11. Think about the life of your family when you were a child. What family rituals were important to you? Which ones have you continued in your own family? What are new family rituals you have created?

❸

IMPRINTS OF FAITH

A family, in preparing their four-year-old son for the birth of a new baby, told him that this child would be a blessing from God. After the birth a friend was over visiting the family and noticed the four-year-old leave the room. The child went into the room where his new baby sister was sleeping and was heard to say to her, "Now, can you tell me what God looks like?"[1]

It's a common yearning, to be in God's presence, to know God face-to-face. People of every faith tradition share in the quest to know God, to explore the mysteries of God's presence. In the Hebrew Scriptures, there are numerous stories of people seeking God's face. Moses was one of those people, and he had seen God face-to-face. Moses asked God what he should tell the Israelites when they asked the name of God, and God told Moses, "I AM WHO I AM." (Exodus 3:14 is also translated "I will be what I will be.") The psalmist expressed in poetry the longing for God:

As a deer longs for flowing streams,
    so my soul longs for you, O God.
My soul thirsts for God,
    for the living God.
When shall I come and behold the face of God? (Ps. 42:1–2)

"AS A LITTLE CHILD"

Upon reading the Gospel stories, we know that this yearning for God did not diminish after Jesus' incarnation. Recall the stories of people who listened to him in face-to-face situations, talked with him, watched him, and wanted to know more—the Samaritan woman, Zacchaeus, a boy with five loaves and two fish, the bent-over woman, the rich young ruler, Mary and Martha, and countless others. And of course, there were the parents of children.

The Gospel writers Matthew, Mark, and Luke told the story of parents who wanted to bring their children to Jesus so that he might touch them and offer a prayer. For some reason the disciples tried to prevent that from happening. They must have mistakenly thought that Jesus was far too busy to take time to hold a child. Perhaps they believed that there were far more important things for Jesus to be doing than praying with parents and children. When Jesus saw what the disciples were doing, he told them, "Let the little children come to me; do not stop them; for it is to such as these that the realm of God belongs."

Jesus' admonishment was enough to make the disciples stop for a minute and think about the meaning of what had happened. But there was more for the disciples and the parents to hear, and Jesus continued, "Truly I tell you, whoever does not receive the realm of God as a little child will never enter it" (Mark 10:14–15). And the One who had time for the least and the greatest and for everyone in between took the children into his arms and blessed them.

In speaking about her move from New York City to Dakota, author Kathleen Norris says, "This is my spiritual geography, the place where I've wrestled my story out of the circumstances of landscape and inheritance. The word 'geography' derives from the Greek words for earth, and writing about Dakota has been my means of understanding that inheritance and reclaiming what is holy in it."[2]

I believe that children are naturally curious about the mysteries of God. The gift of being with children is that we have opportunities to hear perspectives on faith and God from those who are closer to those mysteries of birth and beginnings of life than we are. In making a home for faith for children, families have the opportunity to provide a spiritual landscape, or geography as Norris calls it. The inheritance of faith is passed on to another generation.

Essential in understanding the notion of a child's being imprinted with faith is Jesus' teaching that receiving and entering his realm is possible only to those who do so "as a little child." This chapter will give you the opportunity to think about children, their development, and the kinds of things they need from caring, faithful, and loving adults in their families.

"CLAIMING OUR EPIPHANIES"

Christopher asked his mother if God made "griffins." "Did he? Did he? Did he?" he asked. Everything has to be repeated at least three times these days.

"No, I don't think she did," his mother answered.

"Is God a *girl*?" was the next question as she knew it would be.

"I think God is everything girls are and everything boys are," his mother answered.

Christopher asked his mother, "Is God big?"

She responded, "Yes, I think God is very big."

"He must be a giant," Christopher said. "Where does God walk?" asked Christopher.

And his mother asked him, "Do you think God walks around on the earth?"

Christopher answered, "He walks all around and steps on the houses. He is invisible. I think he walks on the oceans so he won't step on anyone. God's invisible." It's a beautiful day and Christopher opens his car window. The wind is blowing in, and it feels like spring. "God is invisible like the wind. God is the wind."

"I feel God giving us a hug," his mother says.

Christopher thinks this is really silly. "God's not the wind," he says. "God is a person."

The title for this section of the chapter emerged from my reading of Kathleen Norris's book *Cloister Walk*. She wonders how or why we "become exiled from the certainties of childhood."[3] What happens to the creative and expressive theologians who are our children? Why do many of them often leave church at the first opportunity they have to make their own decision? "I wonder if children don't begin to reject both poetry and religion for similar reasons, because the way both are taught takes the life out of them. If we teach children when they're young to reject their epiphanies, then it's no wonder that we end up with so many adults who are mathematically, poetically, and theologically illiterate."[4] In thinking about the combination of reason and imagination that she says "bring[s] us up against our true abilities and limitations,"[5] Norris offers an assessment of this "curious mess," as she calls it.

> We've grown afraid of the imagination (except as a misguided notion of a "creativity" granted to a few) and yet are less and less capable of valuing rationality as another resource of our humanity, of our religious humanity. We end up with a curious spectrum of popular religions, a rigid fundamentalism at one end, and New Age otherworldliness, manifested in "angel channeling workshops," on the other. . . . What gets lost in all of this is any viable sense of the sacred that gives both imagination and reason room to play.[6]

For Norris, "poetry, like prayer, is a dialogue with the sacred. And poets speak from the margins, those places in the ecosystem where, as an ecologist can tell you, the most life forms are found."[7] So how do we nurture children as poets? What can parents do to encourage a kind of religious imagination that becomes a scaffolding for faith that will see them through the coming years when rational questions of why and why not replace mysterious wonderings about God and God's being in the world?

Reread Deuteronomy 6. Recall the place where we are to keep the great commandment to love God—in our hearts. Later in Deuteronomy 30, Moses continued to remind the people that God would see them through the wilderness to the promised land. He reminded them of the commandment, that it is neither too hard nor too far away from them: "The word is very near to you; it is in your mouth and in your heart for you to observe" (Deut. 30:14). When asked about the coming of God's realm, Jesus responded in a similar way. It would not come in ways that someone could look and say, "'Look, here it is!' or 'There it is!' For, in fact, the realm of God is among [or within] you" (Luke 17:21).

Reflecting on my childhood, I think seeds of theological literacy were planted very early. Four things enabled their being embedded in my life so that a scaffolding for faith was in place, one that would see me through adulthood. I was born into a loving family. I was the first grandchild on both sides of my family and was held, loved, and tenderly nurtured within an extended family of grandparents, aunts, and uncles.

I was also born into a faithful family, active in the life of a congregation. A few months after I was born, I was baptized. In writing about this occasion my father recalled how I screamed through it, and nothing they did would console me. "As we beat a hasty retreat, someone whispered, loud enough for all pew neighbors to hear, 'maybe the little dear just didn't want to become a Presbyterian.'"[8]

Going to church school on Sunday with my family was an important ritual in our lives that began when I was two, old enough to go to my first "class" at church. My parents lived out the promises they made at my baptism, and the church became another place in which I was at home.

I was born into a family of readers. So it is not surprising that one of the things that stands out in my memory as an evening ritual is reading a book. My parents read children's stories to me every night. A book that became part of my own evening ritual after I learned to read was a Bible storybook. I loved to read the stories again and again. There weren't many pictures in the book, but the stories were alive and colorful in my mind.

The last piece of scaffolding that has sustained my faith is different from the other three. It's not as much a practice or a context as a theological affirmation. My mother is a gardener. She loves nothing better than to spend her spring and summer days working in the soil, planting, tending the vegetables. Her faith in God is deeply connected with her understanding of creation and the created world. I learned early in my life that earthworms are not "yucky, slimy things" but important creatures in God's world. My mother told me that they were important in aerating the soil and finding them was a good sign of the health of the garden.

"Thank you, God, for earthworms," she said. I have never grown to love holding earthworms as much as my mother does, but I believe that a foundation for my theological epiphanies was established very early by the connections my mother made with the earth and its seasons and the world God created. The natural rhythms of birth, life, and death were observed first in nature. Knowing God first as Creator established an elementary step for the scaffolding that would follow as I learned about larger concepts such as the Trinity and the roles of God as Redeemer and Spirit or Sustainer.

Children are able to claim their epiphanies if they have been given space and the opportunity by caring and faithful adults to express their wonderings, ask their questions, and acknowledge their doubts.

A spiritual life is not something we begin to lead—or to cultivate in our children—after analyzing every book in the Bible, or resolving to be do-gooders, or even deciding we believe in God. Spirit is our life's breath. . . . Spirituality is not something we need to pump into our children, as though it were nitrous oxide at the dentist's. Like oxygen, it is freely available to each of us at every moment of life. Spirit is in every breath we draw and so is spiritual nurture.[9]

Like my mother, Jean Grasso Fitzpatrick believes that it is in the everyday actions of life that we reveal our spiritual selves to children and in so doing we provide space and context for the emergence of their epiphanies: "As we share our reverence for the natural world, the simple joys of family life, our dependability, and our unconditional love, we show them the face of God."[10]

"CELEBRATIONS OF LIGHT"

A child was born prematurely and spent the first hours of his life fighting to live. He's now school age, still quite small for his age, but very healthy. When he was four he told his mother, "I'm getting worried because I'm beginning to forget what God looks like."

Many families have a door frame in the kitchen that looks a bit different from others in their home. This particular one has pencil marks on it, beginning near the bottom and at differing heights up the frame. Marking growth of a child in this way becomes a family ritual. Other families mark growth in another way, with the lighting of a special candle on the anniversary of a child's baptism. Remembering the promise of parents and a congregation to nurture a child in the life of the Christian faith is marked with a celebration of light.

Through their research, developmental theorists have provided background that helps us understand the growth in a child's life represented by pencil marks and lighted candles.[11] When considered together, these theories help us identify the behaviors and tensions present at different stages of growth from birth through adolescence.

A child's growth in faith has been the concern of religious educational theorists for more than one hundred years. Recall the words of Horace Bushnell and his concern for natural growth. Sophia Fahs, a religious educator in the early part of the twentieth century, also contributed to a growing body of knowledge about children and faith.

> When a three-year-old child stands, wondering, before the crushed form of the turtle in the road and asks his questions about death and life, his religious search has begun. Mrs. Fahs suggested that the companionship of an older person in that search is a better security than absolute answers about what happens after death and about the existence of God. The process of religious education can then become a process of questioning, experimenting, studying the variety of answers that [people] have found.[12]

Based on her research and study of young children and the ways that they represent God, Ana-Maria Rizzuto has identified three theses. She found that by the age of six, all children have constructed some image or representation of God. Second, she affirms that the representation of God that the child has developed is drawn from the parent/s or other family members who are important in the child's life. Third, "the representation of God takes form in the space between parents and the child."[13] This same space is occupied by transitional objects such as teddy bears or blankets, the things that comfort children and remind them of the constancy of love, trust, and security. Rizzuto believes that occupying this same transitional space as a beloved bear or blanket, a child's representation of God becomes another way to express consistent love, trust, and faith.

A friend of mine was interested in how her six-and-one-half-year-old daughter was thinking about God. She engaged her in conversation and asked her if she would be willing to draw a picture of God. Her daughter didn't think she wanted to do that, and she went off to play. Later she came back and obviously had changed her mind. She brought with her a crayon picture of her drawing of God. It was a stick figure with a line drawn partly down the middle of the person. In the right hand, God held a flashlight. In the left hand, God was sending down rain. In discussing the picture with her mother, Kristin told her, "I'm not sure if God is a man or a woman; maybe God is both, so God's holding a flashlight in one hand for light and makes rain with the other hand."[14] Kristin has been raised by parents for whom language about God is important. It is natural that her picture represents the thinking about God that she shares with her parents.

In considering the volumes of research that contribute to our knowledge about growth and growing in the life of faith, we may be caught up in the theory to the extent of never getting to the practical questions: So how do I help my child? What can I do?

There are three ways to make connections between theories of child development and the role of parents as primary faith educators. From these particular angles of vision, parents may reflect on the experiences, questions, and struggles, the interior marks of growth that are embedded in the pencil lines on the door frame marking visible signs of physical growth. John Westerhoff describes the needs of children as they grow in faith. Robert Kegan provides a way of understanding the environment in which human beings live, from which they separate and to which they return. To the thinking of these two educators, I add thoughts on the parenting for faith expression needed at differing stages of a child's development.

John Westerhoff offers a simple way of describing the life of faith of children and young people in terms of experience, affiliation, and searching.[15] He believes that the concrete experiences of being taken to church as a small child, saying prayers together, having blessings at meals, reading stories together, and helping someone else contribute to the foundations of faith. As a child enters school, her or his world broadens to include more people, more ideas, more life experiences beyond the home and neighborhood. A child affiliates with more people and groups in the culture and begins to learn their stories and traditions. A searching faith is that of an older child or adolescent who asks tough questions about faith and God.

Robert Kegan is an educator who has said that human beings live and grow in "cultures of embeddedness," which have three functions. They hold on to us, let go of us and remain in place, or are reestablished in times of change or transformation.[16] These cultures of embeddedness are with us throughout our life spans as we move back and forth between the tasks of separating, forming self and identity, and integrating, relating to others.

Kegan's concept is easily illustrated by remembering how a child learns to walk. A child first learns to stand by holding on to a hand or an object such as a chair or short table. Have you ever watched a child standing in front of a coffee table playing with a toy? Sometimes the child needs both hands and, without realizing it, lets go and is able to balance without holding on to anything. The next step comes when the child lets go and takes a step. A loving parent is there with open arms in case the child falls. Walking requires a child to first let go of what she is holding on to. Sometimes in walking away, a child forgets where the parent is and immediately walks to find the parent and return "home" to his or her arms.

Kegan's cyclical understanding of development is helpful in thinking about the role of parents in relating to the faith needs of a child, which change over time because of development and life experiences. A third concept integrates the reality of a child's development and the involvement of parents. The reality of development is change. As a child grows from infancy to toddler, from being a young child who looks at the experiences of life in concrete terms to a preadolescent who is able to deal with abstract conceptual thinking, the role of parents in caring for the child changes with each phase of the child's development. The parents' role as faith educators also adapts with the child's faith needs.

Consider the practice of prayer. A mother nursing her child silently prays for his health and his future. A father, kissing his daughter on the head as he covers her with a blanket, offers a prayer of thanksgiving to God for her life and her presence in his life. As a family sit down for a meal, they hold hands, and everyone joins in singing the blessing. The youngest child is not yet able to say all the words, but he knows that holding hands begins the prayer. Sitting with her family in worship, a third grader is prepared to participate in worship because she has been learning how to pray at home. Bedtime prayers of thanksgiving and intercession are ones she recognizes in worship. With the help of church school teachers and her parents, she has learned to say and to begin to understand the Prayer of Jesus. A fifth grader takes communion with his family and is able to connect the prayer of thanksgiving used before the sacrament with family table blessings he has said and sung for all the years of his life.

Another example illustrates Westerhoff's guidelines for sharing faith with children, that of being involved in faithful acts of service. A family has a ritual of spending time outdoors in community parks. Warm weather picnics and chances to play on swings and slides are eagerly awaited by the two-year-old. Parents notice trash on the playground and pick it up. Soon the child starts picking up trash as well. After participating in this ritual for some time, the now three-year-old child asks, "Why? Why do people throw down their trash?" And a parent is ready and able to answer the question and to talk about God's world and our role as caretakers, stewards of God's creation. The elementary age child helps with the Saturday ritual of gathering up newspapers, glass, and plastic to take to the recycling center. Developing a theology of the earth begins with participating in acts of caretaking. The role of the parent shifts back and forth between role model and discussion partner, one able to make connections between acts and faith.

A child grows up before our very eyes. The pencil marks on the door frame are visible reminders of the many changes in a life. Lighting the baptismal candle on the anniversary of this date recalls for us more invisible ways a child has grown in faith, before our eyes. We light the candle, add fresh pencil marks on the door frame, and offer our prayers for a child in hope that she or he will never forget God's place in her or his life.

EVERY CHILD NEEDS

On Saturday Dec. 7, approximately 30 people (elementary youth, parents and siblings), convened at Second Harvest Food Bank to sort food for hungry people in Nashville. If you've never been to Second Harvest, it is quite an experience! Long tables are covered with empty boxes; signs hanging from the ceiling indicate where to place peanut butter, baby food, green beans, etc. The kids seem to have a favorite category—"novelty," a miscellaneous category for Jell-O, cake mix, and anything else without a category of its own. Everyone is running around, grabbing food from the big boxes of donated items and placing them in the appropriate categories. One of the children approached an adult, held up a box of Jell-O and asked, "Is this nativity?" "Yes, she answered, this is nativity." God made flesh. The love of God made visible in the caring hands of children.[17]

A few years ago Chicago's public television station produced and aired a show titled *10 Things Every Child Needs*. Through conversation with child development specialists, pediatricians, parents, child care professionals, and teachers, these things were identified as essential to a child's growth: interaction, touch, stable relationships, a safe, healthy environment, self-esteem, quality child care, communication, play, music, and reading.[18]

Watching that show reminded me of how simple yet important this list is. There are no surprises on the list. What caught my eye was the reality of the common things parents do on a daily basis and the contribution they make to the essentials required for a child's healthy growth and development. This list caused me to wonder about another list:

10 Things Every Child Needs from Faithful Parents

1. Parents who are at home with their faith, ones who feel comfortable using God language, reading the Bible, and praying with their children.

2. Caring adults who can help children make connections between faith and life.

3. Participation as a family in the life of a congregation, making commitments to keep sabbath. Honoring sabbath, a day of rest, helps children learn about rhythms of life, work, and rest. Sabbath can be observed in simple ways such as doing things together as a family.

4. Parents who can support connections between church school, worship, and the life of faith at home by retelling Bible stories, singing songs and hymns, and saying prayers.

5. Experiences with other faithful adults. The reality of many people today is that they live apart from their extended families. Seeing relatives across the life span often happens only

occasionally. Inviting adult friends from church, the neighborhood, or work to be involved in the life of your child is a benefit both to the child and to the adult.

6. Opportunities for experiences with people of other cultures and faith traditions. Growing up experiencing and appreciating difference rather than shutting oneself off from it is essential for living in this new century.

7. Keeping/living the faith at home, following the liturgical calendar, rituals of faith and learning. Making a home for faith assumes that practices and meanings of the church year can be reinforced at home.

8. Books to read and to be read from.

9. Time/space for questions, wonderings about the mystery of God, opportunities for creative expression—music, art, drama, words.

10. Time, patience, and love.

EVERY PARENT NEEDS

A parent wrote her pastor in anticipation of her son's baptism. "I know it will be a busy day, with the other babies and happy parents there, too. So I want to tell you in advance; thank you for initiating our son into the world, for bathing him in hope."[19]

Just as children have basic faith needs, things they can expect of parents, family, and other adults in their lives, parents have faith needs as well. These things contribute to their ability to be at home with their faith and to their formation as primary faith educators with their child. These guidelines are written from my perspective as religious educator, teacher, pastor, and theologian. The list has evolved over time spent with parents, pastors, and religious educators. Parents want to know they are doing something right. Pastors and educators want parents to understand that educating for faith is a partnership between the church and the home.

This list could provide a beginning point for parents and pastoral leaders to discuss the kind of preparation that is needed for parents to feel at home with their faith. Having conversations about the guidelines in a setting with other parents is another way to make use of them. Parents and other family members can use this list for their own reflection and think about which ones are most essential.

A word of caution: don't be overwhelmed by this list. It contains several kinds of abilities. Some are skills that can be learned, some focus on a way or style of being with children, some are practices, and some challenge thinking, attitudes, and assumptions. Remember, everything does not need to be accomplished tomorrow.

1. Parents can read a story from the Bible. This assumes a basic familiarity with the Bible, its organization, content, and time line. It also assumes an ability to judge the appropriateness of stories for children, according to their age. In commenting on using the Bible with young children, Elise Boulding, a Quaker, has said, "Knowledge of Scriptures has never cramped a child's spirit, the cramping comes only through the lifeless rendition of Scriptures by uncomprehending adults."[20] In reflecting on the tension between reading the Bible and integrating it, Jean Grasso Fitzpatrick believes that "the stories we can share most effectively are the ones that mean something in our own lives."[21]

2. Parents can tell a Bible story. I am concerned that a vanishing ability of adults today is that of storytelling. During many moments in a day or evening, a story that someone tells, not reads, is appropriate. This ability assumes familiarity with a biblical text. The only way to learn a story is to read it, sit with it for meaning and understanding, and then practice telling it. An excellent resource for those who want to develop this skill can be found in Thomas Boomershine's *Story Journey.* (See appendix 3 for more help.)

3. Parents can deal with children's questions. Notice the particularity of the language here, "deal with." Being available to hear and have conversations with children is more important than always being able to provide a "correct" answer. As Marc Gellman and Thomas Hartman point out in their guidelines that follow this list, it is fine to say, "I don't know," or "I don't know, but why don't we think about it together."

4. Parents can pray (privately and publicly). Individuals have differing levels of comfort with prayer, in private, in family settings, or in public settings. A level of comfort with prayer is closely connected to the first thing on this list, reading a Bible story. If adults are afraid of making a mistake or revealing lack of knowl-

edge or experience with traditions of the faith, then most likely they will not attempt to pray in public or family settings. Here children can be our teachers. Simple prayers with children help us learn about how to pray prayers of adoration, thanksgiving, intercession, and confession.[22]

5. Parents can take some time during a day or a week for personal meditation, Scripture reading, journaling, and being with/listening for God. The form for personal meditation or being with God will be different for each person. When my sister was focused on being at home with her three small children, she referred to her "five minutes of peace." I was reminded that for busy parents, five minutes alone in the shower might be all of the time available in a busy day. Finding a time will change as the family changes. What is important is to recognize the ways a life of faith is nurtured and take steps toward including it as a practice.

6. Parents can ask faith questions. Engage work, the newspaper, and the Christian faith. The theologian Karl Barth believed that it was important to have the Bible in one hand and the newspaper in the other. Reading them together, he believed, was essential for the integration of the Bible and a faithful life lived in the world as a Christian. Thinking about the events of the day and understanding them from theological perspectives are essential for parents who seek to enable faith expression of their child.

7. Parents can struggle to understand and interpret affirmations of faith while recognizing the balance between the doing of a life of faith in mission and witness and the being of faith in meditation, Scripture, reading, and prayer.[23] Here the concern is with balance in a life of faith. On any given day, week, or month, there are opportunities for helping a child name God's presence in the world and act in light of this faith. A simple affirmation, "God loves you and I love you," helps a child understand in concrete ways the meaning of love as she or he experiences it from a parent. Then a connection can be made to another affirmation, "God wants us to love other people." And love takes the form of caring acts for others.

8. Parents can explain the meaning of the sacraments and the liturgical year to their child. In Deuteronomy 6:20, the retelling of the story of God's people follows the statement, "When your children ask you in time to come, 'What is the meaning of . . . ?'"

When a child asks, "Why is the minister putting water on his head?" or "Is this the Sunday we get snacks in church? I like that; why don't we get them every week?" or "The minister calls this a meal; it's not really a meal. What is it?" a parent should be able to answer these questions with simple answers. Sometimes answering theological and sacramental questions with simple and concrete answers is more difficult than longer, abstract theological responses. But it's important for parents to feel comfortable being theologians with their children "when they ask."

A family's connection to the seasons of the church year in their life at home reinforces learnings from church. Knowing that Advent, Christmas, and Epiphany are followed by Lent, Holy Week, and Easter and then Pentecost helps children make connections between seasons of the earth, cultural holidays and celebrations, and traditions of the church and the Christian faith.

9. Parents can struggle with language for God. Maria Harris has said, "Names and meanings of God need to be appropriate, appropriate to God, and able to be appropriated by us and our children."[24] In a wonderful book for people of all faith traditions, *In God's Name,* Sandy Eisenberg Sasso tells the story of people arguing about God's name. Some call God Shepherd; others call God Rock, Healer, Redeemer, Comforter, Father, Creator of light, or Mother.[25] This book helps parents explore their understandings and experiences in addressing God. Being open to the many biblical names for God enables our continuing growth in relating to the mysteries of God and God's transcendence and immanence in our lives.

10. Parents can realize the importance of becoming familiar with basic beliefs and religious practices of other faith traditions in the world. I was reading an article about a Hindu worshiping community in the newspaper, and it reminded me of pictures I have seen from other cultures. Their places for worship have no chairs or pews because in worship when they pray, they get down on their knees. I knew about their practice of prayer but had not made the connection that there would be no places for sitting because of that worship tradition.

Increasingly, the world of our children is a world of diversity of cultures and faith traditions. Celebrations in schools in December now focus on Christmas, Kwanzaa, and Hanukkah. The commitment of parents to learning about other faith traditions with their children is essential in enabling children to know why and how they are different from and similar to others with regard to faith and beliefs.

11. Parents can be regular participants in adult religious education. Opportunities to converse with other adults are beneficial for parents. Many churches offer classes or small groups in varieties of contexts and times over a year. Participation in a Bible study or contemporary issue in dialogue with other adults across the life span nurtures the life of faith. The congregational model of church school for all ages and worship for all ages rather than church school for children offered at the same time as worship for adults makes it possible for parents to participate in these two essentials for nurturing a person in the life of the Christian faith.

12. Parents can be participants/lay leaders in worship. Being in worship provides moments of focus, quiet reflection, participation in the rituals, a chance to hear God's Word and contemplate its meaning for a life in faith. Participating in worship with your child may mean that some of these things may be possible and others may not, based on a child's needs and abilities. A commitment to observing sabbath and making space to participate actively in the worship life of a congregation is significant for ones seeking to be at home with their faith. Many churches offer opportunities for laypeople of all ages to be involved in the planning and leading of worship. Serving as a lay liturgist or lector who reads the biblical text is a way of leading in worship.

This list of twelve guidelines for parents should provide a starting point for consideration of faithful practices that are or could become a part of your life. In their book *Where Does God Live? Questions and Answers for Parents and Children,* Rabbi Marc Gellman and Monsignor Thomas Hartman provide another list of suggestions for parents' "Godtalk," which is their word to describe a parental conversation with children about God. They believe it is important to do the following: (1) "Let your child watch you do the religious things you do. (2) Tell your children what you believe, while making it clear to them that they must decide for themselves what they believe. (3) Don't be afraid to say, 'I don't know' when talking to your child about God. (4) Try to relate God to how we live, not just to what we believe. And (5) Don't give answers about God which are too simple."[26]

"THE CIRCLE OF DAYS"

> For brother sleep, and sister death, Who tend the borders
> of our breath. . . . For all your gifts, of every kind, We
> offer praise with quiet mind. Be with us Lord, and guide
> our ways around the circle of our days.[27]

The connection Kathleen Norris makes between theological illiteracy and the ways we teach young children "to reject their epiphanies" is an important one. It is essential that our children learn the stories of faith, the liturgical words used in worship, hymns, and songs of faith.

Equally essential is helping parents understand that being with their children in affirming faith, living faith, and naming faith—the informal theological epiphanies that happen every day—teaches and empowers a life of faith in ways as essential as formal schooling in the church. Together as partners, it is possible to raise children in faith so that their theological epiphanies are affirmed and nurtured.

A few days after his conversation about God and where God walks, Christopher had this conversation with his mother. "Are all children people?" he asked her. "Yes," she said, "all children are people." "Well," he asked, "are all people children?"

Christopher's question is the point Jesus was trying to make with his disciples. The imagination of children intersects with the reasoned thinking of adults. In our decision to make room in our lives for children, we also make commitments to being surprised on a daily basis with the imprints of faith that are present within "the borders of our breath." Being there as parent, grandparent, godparent, aunt, uncle, or friend to help a child name and claim his or her theological epiphanies is our responsibility and our joy.

QUESTIONS FOR REFLECTION AND DISCUSSION

1. Consider your childhood. What ideas about God have contributed to your belief system? Who or what was most formative in your earliest experiences of thinking about God?
2. What would you like to add to the list of "10 Things Every Child Needs from Faithful Parents"?
3. As you look over the list of parental expectations, where are your strengths and weaknesses?

4. For an activity with a group of adults, take turns naming Bible stories that stand out in your memory from childhood. Which of these stories are still important to you today? Why? This same activity may be done with children.

5. This story has been floating on the Internet. With a group of adults, discuss the biblical texts that are implicit in this story. Rewrite the story using other characters, including women.

The Bible in 50 Words (Read Down)

God made,	people walked,	love talked,
Adam bit,	sea divided,	anger crucified,
Noah arked,	tablets guided,	hope died,
Abraham split	Promise landed,	Love rose,
Joseph ruled,	Saul freaked,	Spirit flamed,
Jacob fooled,	David peeked,	Word spread,
Bush talked,	prophets warned,	God remained.
Moses balked,	Jesus born,	
Pharaoh plagued,	God walked,	

—Anonymous

6. Using Boomershine's guidelines for telling a Bible story (see appendix 3), practice learning and telling one story from the life of Jesus. If you are discussing this chapter with a group of adults, each person could volunteer to tell a story. Discuss what you learned in this exercise.

4

"And When Your Child Asks"

After Moses reminded the Israelites of the greatest commandment, to love God with all their heart, their soul, and their strength (Deut. 6:4–9), he related the word from God to the reality of their lives: "When your children ask you in time to come, 'What is the meaning of the decrees and the statutes and the ordinances that our God has commanded you?' then you shall say to your children . . .'" (Deut. 6:20–21). And Moses instructed God's people to remember the story of the time in Egypt and their deliverance by God. They came to understand that in the telling and retelling of their story, they would remember God and recall God's presence with them even in times of despair, doubt, confusion, wandering, and settling in new homes.

When a child asks you a faith or God question, what do you do? Sometimes you want someone else present to help with the answer. On some occasions an answer is not as important as responding, "What do you think?" And many times a direct answer is just what is needed. What is going on with children and their faith questions? What does a parent need to know in order to be comfortable with a child's question?

This chapter begins with some reminders about what we know about children and their development. Recalling what we already know helps adults to make connections between the children's questions and their differing stages of growth. A quick look at children's questions helps us to understand some of the questions behind the questions. Finally, this chapter introduces you to some "experts," people writing books about kids' questions. Take a moment and recall your earliest memories of questions and curiosities about God. When did you begin wondering about God?

KIDS AND QUESTIONS

Why? What makes the clouds move? Why do people hurt each other or animals? Where does God live? Does God love my teddy bear? Can I see God? What does God look like? Why does God let a tornado kill people? Why did my friend's mommy have to die?

When a child asks such questions, how do you respond? Moses was clear that when children ask, adults were supposed to be able to respond with a story that would help them understand about who they were in relation to God and God's creation. In one sense, children's questions are timeless because they relate to their developmental stage of thinking. Many questions are predictable, and so we can think ahead about our responses. In another sense, the questions that children ask are more complicated because of the times and locations in which we live.

In their book *Engaging in Transcendence,* Bill and Barbara Myers speak of the toxic nature of the world in which children live. As we see and read of the growing numbers of abused children, of schools spending more money on metal detectors than books, of families torn apart by the ravages of war, separation, and divorce, we know and understand that the space surrounding children today is often inhospitable. It can be deadly. In their book *The War against Parents: What We Can Do for America's Beleaguered Moms and Dads,* Sylvia Ann Hewlett and Cornel West discuss the "poisonous popular culture" in which children are being raised today and the effect on parents: "The zeitgeist of contemporary American culture has become profoundly antagonistic toward parents. Moms and dads are attacked, blamed, disparaged, and undercut to a degree that is quite staggering, and our all-encompassing media are on the leading edge."[1]

God knew that the Israelites would need to tell and retell to their children the story of God and God's presence with them. Faithful adults in our time need similar leadership: "To 'lead' assumes a vision, and those who educate from within a religious tradition lean—with spirited hope—into the future because of and in response to such a vision. God is present here. As religious educators, we can and should invoke sacred space. And, in this process, transformation, surprising and uncontrolled occurs. The holy is encountered in our shared experience and our very being."[2]

In this quote are embedded the guidelines for any adult or parent who seeks to be a faith educator, a faithful educator with a child. The first claim such an adult needs to make is: *I am a religious educator with my child.* In making that affirmation, an adult is saying yes to a role, one that is in partnership with the church and church school teachers, the pastor and other Christian educators.

A second guideline sustains the role of adults and parents as religious educators: *We listen and respond from within a particular faith tradition,* which forms us, nurtures us, and offers us a vision for God's presence in our lives, the lives of our family members, and the world. We have a story to tell, and when children ask, our experience of faith enables us to respond to the deeply theological questions with which they are struggling.

When we can affirm our role as religious educators and live out of the faith background that sustains us, *we create sacred space* in the moments of our interactions with children. Myers and Myers speak of this sacred space as a place where we are transformed because "the holy is encountered."[3]

Questions that children ask about God and the realities of the world often catch us by surprise because we don't always know the context out of which they arise. A child can think about something for a long time before verbalizing a question. Other times, the question is more immediate, related to an incident or experience of which the adult may or may not be aware.

The preparations for being a resourceful faith educator are not unlike those involved in finding a safe place for a preschool child. Recall the steps involved in seeking a baby-sitter for an infant, locating the right preschool program or child care center. What questions do you ask? What are you looking for in a person or a program? What qualities do you believe are essential for someone who will care for your child? Selecting a school, a program, or a person requires thinking, planning, and considering personal values and priorities, not to mention spending time in on-site interviews/evaluations, filling out application forms, and participating in parent conferences and programs involving the children.

The investment parents make in their own preparations to be present with and for their child requires the same kind of planning and thinking ahead, the "vision" of which the Myerses speak. The research of early childhood educators is helpful in connecting children's religious thinking as it relates to their developmental stage of growth. Reminding ourselves of how children develop cognitively, emotionally, and socially is essential when we add the layer of how children are formed in faith. Adding to the thinking of Rizzuto, Westerhoff, and Kegan from chapter 3, consider here the developmental thinking of Erik Erikson and James Fowler. Their research and writing enable us to learn about the connections between religious awareness and stages of growth in infancy (birth to age one), early childhood (ages two to six), and childhood (ages seven to twelve) and to gain insights about the ways we educate our children in faith, the "clearing for God" that we make available in our family life.

Recall Erik Erikson's theory of how we develop socially and psychologically. Erikson has framed his theory around a series of eight conflicts that characterize different stages of growth. In infancy (birth to age one), healthy development is based on a child's experience of the world as being a place of trust or mistrust. If an infant's experience is one where a loving parent feeds, changes diapers, holds and loves her, she develops in an environment of hope, and knowing that her caregivers and environment are trustworthy, she continues to trust. Imagine the opposite—a child whose caregiving is sporadic, who knows hunger and cold, the absence of touch and kind words—and consider the kind of transitional object for God represented by this child's experience of the world.[4]

Erikson identifies two developmental tasks for early childhood (ages two to six). Two- and three-year-olds struggle with developing a sense of autonomy and the shame or doubt that can arise when trying to achieve this sense of self from parents or caregivers. Rizzuto describes children at age two or two and a half as ones who ask a lot of questions about how things are made. Then at age three they ask questions of causality: Why does the wind move the clouds? Why does the baby grow in the mommy's tummy? You can make the connection between the "clearing for God" we make for children and their questions. If we encourage their questions and their curiosities about God and the world, we help them with their growing sense of autonomy. And the opposite happens if we refuse to allow their questions that are the foundation for their growing sense of a healthy self.

A second struggle of four- to six-year-olds focuses on finding a sense of purpose through taking initiative, making choices. If such initiative is affirmed, a child has a sense of well-being and accomplishment. If a child's attempt to make use of his creativity is not appreciated or encouraged, then a sense of guilt emerges rather than pride. This tension between initiative and guilt should be understood in context. Erikson does not condone all kinds of initiative as being helpful to a child's growth. The emphasis here is on continuing to support a child's developing sense of a strong self and the ability to live in the world and make a difference, a contribution.

Sometimes children's offer to help with a task is not readily welcome to adults because we know we can do it faster and better and neater. But we know that if we let them help us, they learn by doing. Consider their growing sense of initiative in terms of faith identity. Participation in a community of faith that encourages the presence and leadership of children this age contributes to their growing understanding of themselves in relation to God.

James Fowler's research on how faith develops in individuals is closely related to the work of Erikson. Fowler discusses the pre-images of faith of the infant, the intuitive-projective faith of the young child, and the mythic-literal faith of the school-age child. Pre-images of faith, Fowler believes, are nurtured in the "eyes that recognize and the face that blesses" of the parent/s and significant others who surround the child.[5]

The intuitive-projective faith of the child is represented by a child who is surrounded by a world that is new to her, a world where imagination has a place to grow as questions freely emerge and are verbalized. The school-age child longs to hear stories and to know his place in the narrative. Mythic stories of larger-than-life heroes and literal stories of family and self contribute to a growing sense of identity. Identity comes through hearing stories and finding a place in them.

Knowing the developmental journey of our children helps us in understanding the sources and kinds of questions they ask. A basic background in understanding developmental theory can be for an adult like the help window in a computer program. Have you ever been typing along and the little help character appears unbidden and politely suggests you might be having a problem: Would you like some help? it asks.

Being at home with your faith and being comfortable with the queries and wonderings of children are like having that help character pop up when you might not expect it. Trusting in your life experiences and in the "clearing for God" you have made in your life will see you through the myriad observations and curiosities that children remind you of and that you in your adulthood may have forgotten, solved, or moved beyond.

WHAT'S IN YOUR BACKPACK?

> Knowing about God is not like knowing about plumbing (where you really do need to go to a plumbing expert or your house will leak!). You don't have to be a rabbi, priest, or minister to be an expert about God. Lots of people, maybe including your parents, are God experts, and lots of people can teach you about God. The people who are God experts (the people you want to learn from) are any people who have let God into their lives, and who are trying to do what God wants them to do in the world.[6]

According to this definition, are you an expert? I hope so! Marc Gellman and Thomas Hartman wrote these words for children in the introduction to their book *Where Does God Live? Questions and Answers for Parents and Children.* Another rabbi, Harold Kushner, speaking from his perspective in Judaism in the preface to his book *When Children Ask about God,* writes about a theological perspective that emphasizes not "What is God like? But what should we do differently once we have let God into our lives? Theology has been not so much the study of God as the study of human beings tuned into God."[7] Implicit in the thoughts of these three religious leaders are two foci that have been discussed in this book, being with God and living in response to God. What we believe about God impacts how we live in the world.

In chapter 2 you were asked to consider writing a faith statement. This exercise reminds us that if we are interested in nurturing a child in the life of the Christian faith, then it is essential to be able to name and affirm our beliefs. Moments come in the lives of adults when we search for responses to the wonderings and questions of children. Our backpacks of faith can be empty or full. They can be neatly arranged or messy and a bit cluttered. Whatever the inside looks like, it doesn't matter because it represents you and your journey to being at home with faith.

Many times in adult education groups in the church, a person will begin comments with the phrase, "I'm no theologian," and then go on to share his or her viewpoint. The disclaimer makes it possible to venture an opinion or a judgment, knowing that any statement about God is always limited by human understanding and experiences. Yet that limitation and those experiences affirm the importance of connecting Christian doctrine—beliefs about God and God's relation to humankind—to our living of the Christian faith.

Thinking about God and claiming a Christian identity require us to claim our role as theologians. In his book *Christian Doctrine,* Shirley Guthrie defines theology as a way of understanding "the truth about God, human beings, and the world as it is made known, believed, and experienced in Jesus Christ, the Bible, and the church."[8] A theologian, for Guthrie, is "one who thinks and speaks about both the true God and real human beings in the world."[9] Put that definition in your backpack, and remember that you are a theologian.

Guthrie's book *Christian Doctrine* was originally written for adults to read and study in church school settings, and its chapters follow a basic frame for Christian theology: "God and Human Beings," "God the Creator and Creation," "God in Christ and Reconciliation," and "God the Holy Spirit and New Life." Now you say, "Where is the hard stuff—those questions about evil, sin, the nature of God, those questions that children come up with while we're riding in the car?" They are embedded within the basic understandings of the Trinity. A brief look at these four essential components of Christian theology will help us think in systematic ways about our own belief system.

1. God and Human Beings

Read Genesis 1–2; Psalms 8, 23, 33, 77, 90, 103; and the Gospel of Matthew or Luke.

A child asks her father, "Does God know how to tie shoes, Papa?" He responds by telling her that by God's word "the heavens and earth were made." God breathed, and the "stars took their place." And the little girl responds, "Then God must know how to tie shoes."[10]

In telling about the time after God had created the world, the animals, and people, Sandy Eisenberg Sasso writes in her book *In God's Name,* "But no one knew the name for God. So each person searched for God's name."[11] Each person, from his or her particular angle of vision, had a name for God: Source of life, Creator of light, Shepherd, Maker of peace, Rock, Healer, Redeemer, Ancient One, Comforter, Mother, Father, Friend. Each one argued that his or her name for God was right, and all others were wrong. Finally, they looked at one another: "At that moment, the people knew that all the names for God were good, and no name was better than another. Then all at once their voices came together and they called God One."[12]

People of all ages wonder about the nature of God. Many times we agree, and on many occasions, like that described by Sasso, we disagree about who God is and what we can know about God. Guthrie's frame for thinking theologically starts at the beginning with God and creation. Our questions and the questions of children include: Who is God? Where is God? How does God speak to me? and What is God like? They relate to a basic understanding of God's revelation and doctrines of the Trinity, the ways we know God as Father, Son, Holy Spirit, to use traditional language, or God as Creator, Redeemer, Sustainer.

To wonder about where God is and how or if God is acting in the world describes a focus on God's revelation. The tension present in considering God's revelation is clearly illustrated in responses to devastating natural disasters or human tragedies. Some respond, Why did God let this happen? If God is truly God and in charge of the world, then this hurricane would not have killed all these people. Others who experience the same disaster come through affirming their faith and belief in God's presence with them.

Christians affirm that "God exists because God has found us, not because we have found God."[13] When we engage with the abstract nature yet concrete reality of questions related to knowing God and finding God, we focus on God's revelation, which is evident in three ways: the history of the life of Jesus; the Bible, the book of God's self-revelation to humankind; and "the community of people who through the centuries have listened to, proclaimed, and lived by faith in Jesus and the biblical message."[14]

Knowing and understanding God's relationship with human beings require that we have spent time reading the Bible, becoming familiar with God's interactions with God's covenant people in the Hebrew Scriptures. Struggling to understand the nature of God also assumes that we know the stories of the life of Jesus and have worked with interpreting them in light of life today. One of the most unique aspects of Christian theology is the belief in living in community, the church. In affirming faith in God and belief in the saving acts of Jesus Christ as Savior, we publicly make commitments to growing in faith by active participation in a faith community, an active, witnessing, growing congregation.

2. God the Creator and Creation

Read Psalms 105, 107, 121; one of the prophets—Amos, Hosea, Isaiah, or Jeremiah; and the Gospel of Matthew.

One of the stories of creation in Genesis tells of God's first creating the world and the animals and then creating woman and man. In her book for children, *In Our Image: God's First Creatures,* Nancy Sohn Swartz describes the next part of God's creative act. The animals were worried about what would happen to them after woman and man were created.

> God calmed them and said, "Do not be afraid. For I will create man and woman in My image, after My likeness. woman and man shall be partners with Me to care for you and all the world.
>
> "In addition to your gifts, I will give them the gifts of goodness and kindness and love. I will bless them with the ability to understand and to reason, so they can choose between right and wrong. Just as you give to them, they will give to you."
>
> The animals were no longer afraid. They came out from their hiding places and waited to see what God would create. And all of nature waited to see its reflection.[15]

In retelling the story of the Creator and creation, Swartz has identified basic theological themes: the goodness of creation, the

potential of human beings for both good and evil, and the relationships among the creation and with God. More implicit in this
story is the doctrine of sin.

For the subheadings in understanding God as Creator and the
creation, Guthrie asks these questions: "What Are We Doing
Here? The Doctrine of Creation"; "Why Doesn't God Do Some-
thing About It? The Doctrine of Providence and the Problem of
Evil"; "Who Are We? The Doctrine of Human Beings"; and "Why
Don't You Just Be Yourself? The Doctrine of Sin." [16]

Children of all ages ask questions about God's intervention in
creation. We all want to know why, how to understand the nature
and reality of evil in the world, the shadowy side of creation. And
in moments of pain, fear, and gloominess, when the realities of
human nature are laid bare, we seek light. We have faith in God's
providence that "the loving, just and powerful God who first
made humans and earth, continues to uphold, protect, rule over,
take care of—provide for—God's good creation and each one of
us." [17]

Why can't I do what I know I should do? To ask this question
is to raise the issue of the nature of human beings. Guthrie reminds
us that the basic truth of the Christian faith is not "that we are sin-
ners but that we are human beings created in God's image. Sin dis-
torts, twists, corrupts and contradicts this truth, but it does not
change us into something other than what God created us to be." [18]
However we experience the reality of sin, the bottom line is that
"sin always means broken relationships. It means unwillingness to
be what we are as human beings in the image of God, human beings who are ourselves only as we live in community with God and
our fellow human beings." [19]

Thinking about the realities of the goodness of the Creator
and the human nature of the creation is something we all do—
children, young people, and adults. The question that children
may ask the most and the one with which we struggle all of our
lives focuses on God's power as Creator and God's connection
with the creation, or as Guthrie asks it, "Why doesn't God do
something about it?" We all wonder what if, why, why not? Why
can't I do what is good? Why do people do bad things to other
people, to animals, to the earth, God's creation? To be at home
with these faith questions requires that we struggle with our own

attempts to understand the mystery of the God who creates and the creation that lives in response to God.

3. God in Christ and Reconciliation

Read the Gospel of John.

In retelling the story of Jesus' life, children's author Lois Rock concludes with the story of Jesus' death: "Jesus' friends wept. They put him in a grave. It seemed like the end of the story. But three days later when they went to the grave it was empty. Once again, people talked about Jesus. . . . 'They say Jesus gave them a job to do: to tell people that God loves them, to tell people that God forgives them, to tell people that God will give them new life and keep them safe for ever.'"[20]

When asking people to complete the faith statement form included in appendix 2, I am usually confident that a christological statement will not be a problem for any adult who grew up going to church school and worship, reading the Bible or a Bible storybook at home. We have four Gospels that tell the stories of Jesus, and we have the letters and epistles written by those who came after Jesus and worked to keep his memory alive in the early church.

Recall the images or names for Christ. An angel visited Mary and told her she would have a son, and his name would be Emmanuel, which means "God with us." In the Gospel of John, Jesus used metaphors to describe himself: "I am the bread of life, the living bread that comes down from heaven; the light of the world; the good shepherd; the way, and the truth, and the life; the true vine" (John 6; 8; 10; 14; 15).

When we consider God's saving act of death on a cross and Jesus Christ's resurrection, we speak of the doctrine of atonement, which teaches that "it is God who initiates and fulfills the reconciliation between sinful humanity and God. God is the subject, not the object, of what happened on Good Friday."[21] Rather than overwhelm us with the "terror of God's wrath," the atonement should "awaken in us . . . joyful thanksgiving for God's love."[22] Confronting our beliefs about Christ's saving work, we come face-to-face with our sinfulness and our relationships with other human beings.

The liturgy for Christ's table used on communion Sundays often includes the retelling of the story of the risen Christ meeting the disciples on the road to Emmaus. They did not know who this person was, the stranger walking with them. It was in the breaking of bread at a table that "their eyes were opened, and they recognized him" (Luke 24:31). Being reconciled through Christ, we are called to live in peace and reconciliation with others.

In telling this story for children, Lois Rock reminds us that Jesus gave people a job to do. God's atoning work in Christ is not over. It continues in and through us as we respond faithfully with the jobs we have to do.

4. God the Holy Spirit and New Life

Read John 14; Acts 1–4; and the rest of the book as well.

"If there were an Eleventh Commandment, what would it be?" was a question addressed to children from a variety of faith traditions and backgrounds. In thinking about a commandment in relation to other people, this is what they said:

"No grabbing."

"Don't judge someone by the color of their skin."

"Thou shalt not have racism in thy mind or heart."

"Do not be mean or stare at people with disabilities."

"You shall treat men and women equally."

"Feed everyone and eat together."

"Help the poor."

"Thou shalt not hurt one another."

"Stop the violence."

"No bombing just for the heck of it."

"Peace leads to friendship."[23]

When we speak of the part of the Trinity we call Spirit, we remember its presence in the stories of the Hebrew Scriptures and the Christian Scriptures. God's Spirit was at work in creation. God's Spirit is revealed in worship, creativity, and wisdom. After the baptism of Jesus by John the Baptist, Matthew recorded that "the heavens were opened to him and he saw the Spirit of God descending like a dove and alighting on him" (Matt. 3:16).

God's Spirit reminded God's people of whose side God was on. At the beginning of his ministry, Jesus took the scroll of Isaiah and read in the synagogue in Nazareth:

The Spirit of God is upon me,
because God has anointed me to bring good news
to the poor.
God has sent me to proclaim release to the captives
and recovery of sight to the blind,
to let the oppressed go free,
to proclaim the year of God's favor. (Luke 4:18–19)

We celebrate Pentecost, the gift of God's Spirit and the beginning of the church. In thinking about the Spirit, Paul reminds us of spiritual gifts in First Corinthians 12–14: "Now there are varieties of gifts, but the same Spirit; and there are varieties of services, but the same God; and there are varieties of activities, but it is the same God who activates all of them in everyone. To each is given the manifestation of the Spirit for the common good" (1 Cor. 12:4–7).

In considering in more detail the work of God's Spirit in the lives of human beings, we must address the question of how we know we are Christian and what this confession of faith means for our lives. In theological terms, we are speaking about justification and sanctification. Think of all the ways you try to justify yourself—through hard work, through good behavior, through hard self-criticism. The reality of human nature is that these kinds of justification for our existence are never enough: "Justification means that despite the fact that things are not right in our inner lives and our personal relationships, God forgives and accepts us."[24] "Therefore, since we are justified by faith, we have peace with God through Jesus Christ, through whom we have obtained access to this grace in which we stand" (Rom. 5:1–2).

There is a simple solution to all our frantic attempts to be good, to justify our lives. Church reformers such as Martin Luther spoke of justification by faith, not works. It is not a faith that we earn but a gift of God. "Our faith does not force or enable God to love us, but it is our way of acknowledging, receiving, enjoying—and returning—the love that God had for us long before we ever thought of loving God. We are not made right with God by our faith, but we are made right with God through our faith."[25]

It's essential to speak of justification and sanctification together. In my experience in settings for Christian religious education, I find less conversation in the church about sanctification. Guthrie puts it simply, "Justification tells us how a person becomes a Christian. Sanctification tells us how a person grows in the Christian life. . . . Justification and sanctification are related as gift and task, creed and deed, theology and ethics, faith and life, passively receiving and actively giving in return. No one is a Christian until he or she is both justified and sanctified."[26]

A hymn written by Richard K. Avery and Donald S. Marsh, "We Are the Church," has captured the essence of sanctification as it is nurtured in the life of a faith community.[27] The hymn helps children and adults understand that the church is more than a place or a building, and certainly not just a "resting place." The church is actually "a people," called to live out their faith in the world.

An essential context for growing in the Christian life is a faith community, a congregation. It is the place where we come together for learning and for worship, which is our response to God's redeeming activity on our behalf. In worship, we pray, we sing our faith, we hear God's Word, we remember our baptisms, and we share a meal at the table. Each time we come together as a family of faith, we remember the story of God's people and the many places and ways we are called to live in the world working for God's justice, peace, and love.

The basic tenets of Christian theology—God and human beings, God as Creator, Redeemer, and Spirit/Sustainer—provide ways of organizing our theological questions, affirmations, beliefs, and doubts. Knowing what we believe and why we believe is essential for those who would claim the name Christian.

THE QUESTIONS THAT LEAVE US SPEECHLESS

Talking to God is called praying, and what you say to God is called a prayer. Some of the prayers you say to God have never been said before by anyone. These are personal prayers. Personal prayers come straight from your soul, hit your lips on the way out, and go straight on to God. Other prayers have the same words in them each and every time you say them. These are communal prayers. Communal prayers are the prayers that have been written down in the prayer book of a religion. . . . The reason all religions have prayers or chants or meditations is that all human beings need to say four things in their lives. Those four things that all people need to say are: Thanks!, Wow!, Gimme!, and Oops![28]

Meeting in the intersection between theological doctrine and the questions of children requires the ability to listen and to connect abstract questions with concrete examples, and the commitment to hang in with the child when you would really rather say, "Go ask. . . . She'll know." Would that we could all have the ability to answer children's questions with the honesty, humor, and creativity like that of Marc Gellman and Thomas Hartman as they answer the eternal question of how we talk to God.

Four kinds of questions or observations from children are apparent in their wonderings about God and the world. Sometimes these questions cause a parent to freeze like a computer screen, resulting in an inability to trust her or his knowledge, experience, and convictions.

Information questions related to the Bible require a parent to know biblical stories. Who were Joseph's brothers? Why did Miriam put her brother Moses in a basket in the river? What are the names of Jesus' disciples, and what were they doing before they decided to follow Jesus? A parent without a memory bank of biblical knowledge or a sense of being at home with the Bible so as to locate the answers with the child is unable to be of any help. An information question such as, Can I talk to God? requires a simple answer. But it is best understood when examples are given, such as what Gellman and Hartman did with the four kinds of prayers—thanksgiving, praise/adoration, intercession, and confession—or as they name them: "Thanks!, Wow!, Gimme!, and Oops!"

A second kind of question asked by children can be described as *analytical*. The question about violence and killing in the Hebrew Scriptures is a good example. Other examples are: Why do you think Joseph's brothers were so mean to him? Why did Jesus tell so many stories? These questions give evidence that a child is thinking about the meaning behind the biblical story or passage, oftentimes seeking to make sense of its contemporary relevance. These questions provide a wonderful entry into conversations about the biblical stories to which they relate or the life situations out of which they arose.

A third kind of question is *experiential*. It arises out of reflection and observation. The question might not be "religious" in nature, but connections between belief and actions of Christians can be made in conversation and reflection on the incident. A small child was visiting a museum in Washington, D.C., with his family. He saw a man sitting outside the building and stopped to talk with him. The man was homeless and was asking for money. The child turned to his parent and asked if they could give him some money, which they did. As they walked inside the museum, the child asked, "Why is he homeless?"

A family was watching television together when the news reported a terrible accident. Blood donors of a certain type were needed. The children turned to their parent and asked, "What's your blood type?" After telling them it was the same kind that was needed, and looking at their expectant faces, the father said, "I guess I need to go." And he left to give blood at the hospital.

The daily observations and questions of children present many opportunities for conversation about life and its realities and about faith in God that sustains us in times of certainty and doubt, times of joy and grief. Essential in our response to these experiential moments is to remember that the questions and observations of children arise from the new eyes with which they view the world, eyes with which we too once viewed the world.

A fourth kind of conversation in which children engage focuses on their *wonderings about the mysteries of God*. Where does God live? Can I see God? What is heaven like? Where is heaven? These are questions for which they seek answers, but the answers are ones that theologians have been struggling with for centuries. No one right answer works, but wondering with the child encourages continued engagement with thinking about God and the mysteries for which we don't always have nice, neat answers.

It is possible to connect the essential tenets of Christian theology with questions and affirmations of children. Thinking theologically in children's terms helps make abstract theological doctrines concrete in the life experiences we face each day. Look at the chart and consider the statements and the theological concepts they illustrate.[29]

One of my colleagues on the faculty at McCormick Theological Seminary in Chicago had a favorite question for students. It was the "el stop question." The el (elevated train) is coming and the person next to you asks . . . The train will be here in less than two minutes. What do you say? For example, the person at the el stop turns to you and asks, "How do I know what stories to read to my child from the Bible?"

Major Theme	Language of Children
Creation	God makes everything.
	God plans for the world.
	God plans for me/us.
God's self-revelation	God is forever.
	God loves me/us.
	God is good.
	Jesus showed us what God is like.
	God always keeps God's promises.
Sin	Doing wrong disappoints God.
	Doing wrong hurts me.
	Doing wrong hurts others.
Judgment	What I/we do really does matter.
	I/we live with the outcomes of my/our choices.
	God makes me/us able to choose.
Redemption	God forgives me when I'm sorry.
	God loves me all of the time.
	God loves me even when I do wrong.
People of God	The family of God includes early Bible people, the church, us, and the people around the world.
	People of God help each other.
	People of God worship together.
	The church is people.
	I am included in the church.
Faith response	I can forgive others.
	I'm part of God's family.
	I need you, God.
	It's not always easy to be the person God wants me to be.
	I can trust God.
	Thank you, God.
	I love you, God.
	I'm sorry.
	Help me.
	I'll help you, God.
	I'm happy.
	I can love and serve others.
Providence	God plans for a good world.
	God helps me/us.
Hope	I'm growing.
	God is always with me.
	God always keeps God's promises.

As a Hebrew Scriptures scholar, Dr. Robert Boling used the el stop question with his students to help them understand the importance of both the mystery and transcendence of the God who is revealed in the books of the Hebrew Scriptures and the immanence, the nearness of God to us in relating this mystery to the realities of human life. Knowing and understanding are made clearer in the ability to articulate and struggle with the depth of mysteries of God.

My colleague also knew that biblical study—sitting with biblical texts, translating and interpreting them, and wondering about the connections between their historical context and the present day—was essential. Equally important was the ability of meeting the reality of the immediate question, "So what does that story about Jonah and the big fish really mean? And what does it mean for us today?"

Where do those immediate el stop questions come in your experience with children? Perhaps they come as you are in the car, on a walk, at bedtime, or my favorite "tubby questions," the curiosities that are verbalized in moments of playing and relaxing in a bath. The frame that I use for thinking about such questions assumes that children are being nurtured in their faith at home and in the life of a congregation. The best way for us as adults to be prepared for the moments of "speechless questions" is to have thought about our responses.

Rather than attempt to give answers to specific questions, I would like to explore the questions behind the questions as they relate to two theological concepts: God and human life, and understanding God in three ways, the Trinity. A third concept is more of a hodgepodge, considering the questions behind the questions about the Bible, two holy days, and the sacrament of Holy Communion.

1. God and Human Life

Children are curious about life and death and where God fits into that: What happens when we die? Using examples from nature that illustrate the life cycle of birth, life, and death is the easiest way to help a child understand about what follows life. Accidental deaths or deaths caused by violence require careful attention so that children understand cause and effect and how they relate to God.

The reality of evil, of good and bad actions on our part is of importance. Why did Luis and Jeff hurt each other? Why do people throw trash on the ground when they know they aren't supposed to do that? Why do people kill other people? Why do big people hurt children? Helping children deal with the reality of life in our world is essential so that their questions and their fears can be verbalized. Affirming that bad things do happen but God does not cause them is a way to help children understand the reality of actions and responsibility.

Is God a man or a woman? Young children are often curious about what God looks like. Aren't we all? The way in which we answer this question is important so that children don't have to unlearn things later in life. Illustrations of how to answer this question were given in chapter 3. Essential here is thinking for yourself about your image of God. Remember that children think in very concrete terms; adults are capable of more abstract thinking. My favorite answer for this question is an honest "I don't know": "I don't know what God looks like. I don't think God has a body like we do. I like to think of God like a big cloud, always surrounding me, always there like a strong wind to pick me up when I fall, and like a fluffy pillow to lean against when I need something to support me."

2. God, Jesus, and That "Holy Thing, Is It Really a Ghost?"

God as Creator, Redeemer, and Sustainer is language used by some to describe the nature and work of the Trinity. It is a help to adults as we attempt to understand the nature of God and God's relationship with humankind.

As children participate in educational opportunities at church and hear stories from the Bible at home and in worship, they begin to learn about the Trinity. God's work as Creator is a concrete way for children to picture God. The stories of Jesus' birth, life, death, and resurrection are equally explicit. The Spirit is harder to explain. And of course "Holy Ghost" and all the fun connections with ghosts and Halloween make this third part of the Trinity a more challenging one to explain.

The Greek word for spirit is *pneuma* and has a literal meaning of "wind or breath." Helping children to connect spirit with God's presence, something we can't see but is always there like the love of a parent or other family member, is one way to help them relate concretely to this abstract part of the Trinity.

3. Holy Days, Holy Book, and a Special Meal

One of my favorite lenten resources has the title "And on the Third Day What Do You Celebrate?" And a favorite Advent resource is titled "Whose Birthday Is It Anyway?"[30] The rather in-your-face nature of these titles makes one pause to consider attitudes and practices related to the two most important liturgical celebrations: Christmas and Easter. Faced with the competing stories of Santa and Jesus at the manger, a child might ask, "Was Santa at the stable when Jesus was born?" Bunnies, eggs, and baskets are equally challenging to explain in their relationship to the observance of Holy Week as we move to Easter.

These two seasons of the year offer families wonderful opportunities to help children hear two stories, cultural/ethnic and religious. Many excellent children's books explain these seasons and their symbols, and some of them are included in chapter 6. As a family begins to establish its own traditions related to the celebration of Christmas and Easter, keep in mind the meaning of the holidays and some simple yet concrete ways they can be celebrated at home.

Three questions from children make connections between what we learn at church and what we do at home and when we are away from home: What is the Bible? Why am I Christian and not Jewish or Muslim or Hindu? Why do they call it a meal when it's just bread and juice?

Help children learn about the Bible by reading from it or from a Bible storybook. Allow children to hold the Bible, and talk about why it is special—because it tells us stories about God and Jesus and how God's Spirit has been with us for a very long time. Let children see the Bible in the sanctuary and carry a Bible to worship.

Here is an el stop question for you. You and your child are riding in the car, and your child looks over and asks you, "What's in the Bible?" What do you say? Talking about the kinds of writings in the Bible is one way to answer the question. Talking about how we got it or how biblical stories relate to our lives is another way.

Being comfortable with questions about the Bible helps with the question about differences in religions and beliefs. One way to talk about why we are Christian and not Jewish is to explain how our holy book is different—the Christian Scriptures tell stories about Jesus, God's Child, and the beginning of the church.

Being Christian also means that we remember Jesus when we baptize people with water in God's name and we eat a meal together called Holy Communion. The way in which the sacrament of Holy Communion is celebrated in your congregation contributes to children's understanding of and experience with this "meal." The chance to break off a piece of bread and dip it in a cup can become an important way for children to know they are truly a part of a family of faith beyond the family at home. The meal probably looks more like a snack to them and to many adults. Helping children know that it is a way we remember Jesus and promise to try to live as Jesus would want us to with love, care, and justice for all is a verbal connection with the concrete activity of eating and drinking together in God's name.[31]

RESOURCES IN PRINT AND HOW THEY HELP

In preparing for workshops with adults who are interested in being informed faith educators with children, I often give an overview of the books written by "experts." Within the genre of kids, parents, and questions of faith, the literature can be easily divided into four categories. The first group includes books written for children to read. A second group includes Bible storybooks that can be read by an adult to a child and then later read by the child as reading skills are developed. Large chain bookstores as well as smaller locally owned bookstores usually stock a large number of both kinds of books. A third group is less common; the books address children's questions directly and are designed, I think, to be read by a parent and a child together as a way to grow together in understanding God and God's relation with the world and humankind. A fourth group includes books written for parents to help them think about their role in nurturing a child's life of faith.

The first two kinds of resources are described in chapter 6. Here I would like to illustrate the last two categories, books for children and adults. Two of the best books for children are written by Rabbi Marc Gellman and Monsignor Thomas Hartman. In *Where Does God Live? Questions and Answers for Parents and*

Children (Triumph Books, 1991), the authors use the language of children to help them understand the nature of God through answers to questions such as: Is God real?; Where does God live?; What does God look like?; Does God make miracles?; and Does God know what I'm thinking or what I'll do? Questions about the reality of human life in the world God created are stated in terms like these: If God is so good, why is there so much bad? and Why couldn't God let Grandpa die fast without pain?

A second book by Gellman and Hartman is *How Do You Spell God? Answers to the Big Questions from Around the World* (Morrow Junior Books, 1995). This is a most helpful book for children and parents to read together since it addresses the issue of belief from the perspective of the world and its many faith traditions. This book is essential for Christians who live in a world that is increasingly multicultural and multifaith. Basic beliefs of other faith traditions are addressed with simple questions such as: How are religions the same and different? What question does each religion want to answer the most? What are the holy books? When are the holy days? What are the holy times in my life? How should we live? What happens after we die? What are some of the bad things in religions? What are some of the terrific things in religions?[32]

For parents, there are four excellent resources. Three books focus on the spiritual life of the parent that is nurtured and grows in the process of being a faith educator with a child: *Something More: Nurturing Your Child's Spiritual Growth* by Jean Grasso Fitzpatrick (Viking, 1991), *The Faith of Parents* by Maria Harris (Paulist Press, 1991), and *Gently Lead: How to Teach Your Children about God While Finding Out for Yourself* by Polly Berrien Berends (Harper, 1991). The titles of Berends's chapters invite readers to consider their own faith understandings as they think about explaining things to children: "What Dies and What Doesn't"; "The Humdrum Is the Holy"; "Love Thine Enemy"; and "Tough Moments."

A basic how-to book that deals with children's questions is *When Children Ask about God: A Guide for Parents Who Don't Always Have All the Answers* by Harold S. Kushner (Schocken Books, 1989). The four general themes he addresses are questions about God; issues of suffering, evil, and death; the Bible; and "The Vocabulary of Religion"—sin, repentance, and prayer. Kushner concludes his book with a conversation about hope and finding God in the world.

A book similar to Kushner's addresses the parent's role in "introducing your child to God." In *Talking to Your Child about God: A Book for Families of All Faiths* (Bantam, 1990), David Heller addresses the issue of religion and belief in an interfaith family.

A QUILT TO REMIND ME OF HOME

One of the most privileged and peculiarly human tasks we have inherited is that of recognizing and naming God's presence in life. Most people of faith begin that task with some deep, experiential conviction of God's reality. There are mysteries here whose origins reason does little to explain. It is safe to say simply that every experience of God's truth originates in God's gracious self-revealing.[33]

Much earlier in the life of this country, quilts sewn with patchworks of color and texture were both a necessity for warmth and a product of communal commitment. Women gathered to stitch and share stories and have social times together. There is some evidence that for enslaved African Americans, quilt patterns indicated directions for escape to safe places along the Underground Railroad. The directions for finding a safe home were embedded in the stitches and patterns of the everyday quilt that covered the bed.[34]

In her book *The Keeping Quilt,* Patricia Polacco tells the story of a family that immigrated to the United States from Russia. Anna was the daughter, and the only things she had with her from her home in Russia were her dress and her babushka, and the dress was getting too small for her to wear. Her mother got out a basket of old clothes and told Anna, "We will make a quilt to help us always remember home."[35]

Quilts for providing comfort and warmth and for remembering family stories, quilts that show us the way home, what a rich image for thinking about the life of faith we lead with children. In the quote at the beginning of this section, Marjorie Thompson reminds us of the privilege we have "in recognizing and naming

God's presence in life." To live our faith with children is indeed a privilege. A quilt of faith that has been carefully stitched over the lifetime of a child, with new patches added at different stages of growth and questioning, will be there—in times of doubt, in times of wandering, in times of celebration, and in times of fear and hopelessness—for both the child and the adult.

So what quilt square are you working on at this moment? How will it fit in with the pattern? What new color will it add? Will the stitching be right the first time, or will it have to be re-worked? And when your children ask, tell them the stories of faithful people, the stories of God, who is a God of love and justice, compassion and peace. And when your children ask, live the faith with them. God will be with you!

QUESTIONS FOR REFLECTION AND DISCUSSION

1. When did you begin wondering about God? What are some of the earliest questions you can recall?

2. As you think about the basic tenets of Christian theology, God and human beings, and God as Creator, Redeemer, and Spirit, where do you have questions? If you are discussing this chapter with other parents, spend some time with each of the four major theological themes. These questions will help your discussion:

- Read some of the psalms related to the work of God with humankind. In what ways do the psalmists picture God?

- What conditions in the world of the prophets are similar to our place in God's created world today?

- What teachings of Jesus help us understand about who we are in relation to God?

- Where is God's Spirit at work in your life today? In the life of your congregation? What gifts of the Spirit are yours? What gifts of the Spirit are evident and growing in the life of your child?

3. Recall a conversation with a child and a question of curiosity he or she expressed about God. What kind of question was it? What part of Christian theology did it illustrate?

4. What kinds of questions does your child ask? Which ones are easier for you to deal with? Which ones are harder?

5. If you are teaching this book with parents, consider an activity of quilt making. Squares of cloth can be provided that can be stitched or decorated with fabric markers. What symbols sustain your life of faith? What images remind you of your home for faith? Squares of faith can be turned into a quilt by someone in the class or the church who knows how to make a quilt.

6. Read one of the books for children or parents described in this chapter or in chapter 6. With a group of parents, discuss what you find to be most helpful in the book.

5

A FAITHFUL ECOLOGY
AT HOME, AT CHURCH, AND
IN THE WORLD

The Gospel writer Luke told stories of Jesus' teaching and healing prior to his entry into Jerusalem for the last time. If you read chapters 4 through 22 in the Gospel, you get a sense of the urgency of Jesus' time on earth. It is no coincidence that after his baptism by John, Jesus went home to Nazareth and read in the synagogue on the Sabbath the words of Isaiah:

> *The Spirit of God is upon me,*
> > *because God has anointed me to bring good news*
> > *to the poor.*
> *God has sent me to proclaim release to the captives*
> > *and recovery of sight to the blind,*
> > *to let the oppressed go free,*
> *to proclaim the year of God's favor.* (Luke 4:18–19)

One of my favorite characters in Luke's Gospel is Zacchaeus, a man whom Jesus sought to release from a particular kind of captivity. I like Zacchaeus because he seems so real, so human. I also like this story because I vividly recall as a child in church school singing, "Zacchaeus was a wee little man." The story of Zacchaeus in Luke 19 must be read in context. Jesus had been teaching and talking about justice and riches. Just after the story of Jesus and the rich ruler, Luke told the story of Zacchaeus, a tax collector who wanted to see who Jesus was.

You know the story. Jesus spotted him in the tree and said, "Zacchaeus, come down, for I must stay at your house today." And perhaps over a meal at the table in his home, Zacchaeus saw himself and knew what he was expected to do. Through story, parable, and living example, Jesus had a singular focus of confronting people with the reality of his call, helping people hear, reflect on their lives, and live differently. A unity of belief and action was no longer an option; it was a requirement for those who would seek to be his followers.

This chapter focuses on the unity of faith and life as it is nurtured and challenged in the partnership of home and congregation. Working together, families and the church community provide and support an "ecology for nurturing faith."[1] Faith education in such an ecology becomes the shared responsibility of parents and other family members at home and lay leaders, teachers, members, ministers, and educators in the church.[2]

A faithful ecology is formed in both contexts where faith, hope, and love are practiced. We learn to speak by being spoken to, and later we learn rules of grammar. We learn about love by being loved. We learn about God by singing our faith, practicing our faith, praying in faith, and being faithful. James Fowler has observed that in thinking about the order of knowing and learning, "We need doctrine as rules of faith living, once we've already been formed in the deep structure that makes us Christian folk."[3]

We have spent a lot of time to this point focusing on the home and the role of parents as primary faith educators. This chapter shifts to the partnership of home and congregation. In a culture focused on individualism and immediacy, it's essential to consider a faithful ecology that supports our commitments to making a home for faith.

CALLING AND VOCATION

Thus says God, . . .
Do not fear, for I have redeemed you;
   I have called you by name, you are mine.
When you pass through the waters, I will be with you; . . .
when you walk through fire you shall not be burned,
   and the flame shall not consume you.
For I am your God,
   the Holy One of Israel, your Savior. (Isa. 43:1–3)

God comes to us and calls us by name in many times and places. When God told Sarah that she would have a son, Sarah laughed because she was more than ninety years old. She later gave birth to her son, Isaac (Gen. 18:1–15). In defiance of the call or order of the pharaoh, Miriam helped the pharaoh's daughter save the life of her brother Moses, who was hidden in a basket in the river (Exod. 2:1–10). Moses said he couldn't speak for God, and God answered, "I will be with your mouth and teach you what you are to speak." But he said, "O God, please send someone else" (Exod. 4:12–13). Rahab had heard the stories of God, who saved the people through the Exodus, and she hid spies sent by Joshua, the leader of the Israelites, and protected them (Josh. 2:1–29).

Hannah desperately wanted a child. She prayed to God with a request and a promise. If God would bless her with a child, she would give the child back to God. God answered her call, and she dedicated her child to God and gave him to Eli, the priest in the Temple. When God spoke to Samuel, the young boy ran to the priest because he thought Eli was calling him. Eli knew God was calling Samuel and told him, "Go, lie down; and if God calls you, you shall say, 'Speak, God, for your servant is listening'" (1 Sam. 3:9).

When Elijah feared for his life, he escaped to a cave in the mountains. God found him there and sent an angel to get him back on the right track: "Get up and eat, otherwise the journey will be too much for you" (1 Kings 19:7). When God called Isaiah to be a prophet to God's people, Isaiah resisted, "Woe is me! I am lost" (Isa. 6:5). Jeremiah responded to God's call by saying he was too young (Jer. 1:6), and Amos said he was only a sheepherder and a dresser of sycamore trees, "I am no prophet, nor a prophet's son" (Amos 7:14).

God chose Mary and called her to carry and give birth to a child, whose name would be Emmanuel (God with us). God called Zechariah and told him his wife would have a child who would be named John (Luke 1:26–38). Zechariah responded in disbelief and was mute for nine months (Luke 1:5–24). The Samaritan woman responded to Jesus' call and offer of water by saying, "Give me that living water, so I will never thirst" (John 4:1–30). Jesus called children to come to him (Luke 18:15–17). He called Zacchaeus to come down from a tree, disciples to leave their boats and homes, rich rulers to give away their wealth, and Peter to stay with him in the garden (Gospels of Matthew and Luke).

And God calls to us today. Many themes are present in the Bible, but one that I believe is central to both the Hebrew and the Christian Scriptures is that of call. The calls of God's prophets are sometimes in grand contexts but more often in simple surroundings. After hearing God's call, one laughed, one asked God to find someone else, some claimed to be unqualified for the job or too young, and others ran away.

I believe that God's call is still a central theme for those of us concerned with making a home for faith. Adults at the beginning of this new millennium are called to the vocation of being faithful and responsible Christians with children, with young people, in discipleship in the world. And like people in the Bible, we sometimes laugh at the call to this vocation (What me? You've got to be kidding!). We claim our lack of preparation and qualification (I really don't know enough about the Bible to be a teacher), or we attempt to pass it off to someone else (Call someone else; I'm just too busy). And sometimes like Hannah, Sarah, or Elizabeth, we laugh, cry, and pray to God and then step out in faith not always sure of what's ahead but confident that God's presence will be there.

Maya Angelou describes a strong vision of her grandmother, whom she called Mamma. Living in the Depression and caring for a disabled son and two grandchildren often evoked this affirmation of faith from Mamma: "She would look up as if she could will herself into the heavens, and tell her family in particular and the world in general, 'I will step out on the word of God. I will step out on the word of God.' . . . Naturally, since Mamma stood out on the word of God, and Mamma was over six feet tall, it wasn't difficult for me to have faith. I grew up knowing that the word of God had power."[4]

If we believe in God who calls each of us by name, then we grow in faith confident that God who calls us also nurtures us in a life of faith. This process of growing in a life committed to the Christian faith can be understood as a vocation.

We have often associated the concept of vocation with a job or career. It's that question asked of high school or college graduates sometimes framed in this way: "Well, what are you going to do with your life? What's next for you?" John Westerhoff reminds us that for Christians, "vocation is first and foremost our response to God's call to fulfillment. There are times when we ask, 'Do our lives lead anywhere? Are we going someplace?' Our Christian faith explains that the goal of human life is nothing less than life with God."[5]

And this vocation of living in response to God's call in our lives begins at birth or adoption when a family and a family of faith, the congregation, welcome a child with the waters of baptism or the prayers of dedication. Mark Searle discusses vocation in terms of the Christian identity of the family. He argues that such identity is not inherited from parents but takes form and grows within a faithful ecology. An equally responsible partner is the church, called to "affirm, ratify, and nurture" the child's vocation as Christian.[6] It's one thing to verbally respond to the question to the congregation at a child's baptism, "Do you, as members of the church of Jesus Christ, promise to guide and nurture this child by word and deed, with love and prayer, encouraging them to know and follow Christ and to be faithful members of the church?"[7] Living that response with children is a vocational response to God's call to our lives. If we invite them into our lives, then children and young people grow in their lives with God.[8]

Walter Brueggemann has described this vocation in terms of its context within a community of faith. In a congregation, members are called to create a "communal network of memory and hope in which individual members may locate themselves and discern their identities."[9] The church is perhaps the only institution in our culture where people across the life span come together to remember their story and tell new stories of faith. The church is a place, as Brueggemann suggests, of identity, where children, young people, and adults come to know who they are as Christian, name their place in the story, and share their hope and commitments for living faithfully in the world.

The God who calls each of us by name, the God who has promised to be with us at all times, calls us to a vocation of a life of faith. The God whose presence with us is both mystery and grace calls us home to faith.

BIRTHMARKS AND WATERMARKS

O God, you have searched me and known me.
You know when I sit down and when I rise up;

> *you discern my thoughts from far away.*
> *You search out my path and my lying down,*
> *and are acquainted with all my ways.*
> *Even before a word is on my tongue,*
> *O God, you know it completely.* (Ps. 139:1–4)

In a small book written for Catholic parents, Maria Harris speaks of the role of parents as religious educators and how everything they do in some ways is religious education. She believes that parents are engaged in two particular forms of religious education: physical and storied.[10] By physical, she refers to all the experiences of parents with children: "Everything said physically can be a statement about creation, incarnation, promise and hope. Every comforting touch is a statement about love. Every concrete meeting with someone or something in creation lays the ground for living a sacramental life later on."[11] Through story, children learn who they are within the family, the church, the culture, and the nation. Through story, they begin to understand that "life has a shape to it, a form to it. Life has beginnings, endings, freedom, failure, hope."[12]

A child born or adopted into a Christian family has a birthmark of faith. Through experiences in the family and participation in hearing and telling stories, a family makes its imprint of faith on each member. This birthmark, invisible yet visible in experiences and through story, is described by the psalmist: "O God, you have searched me and known me."

A second kind of mark is very visible, the waters of baptism that mark us forever for a life of faith. Affirmations of faith are made by a parent or parents, promises are publicly affirmed by a congregation, prayers are said, the waters of baptism wash over a child's head, and a new life is welcomed into a community of faith. The watermark of baptism is the most visible sign of the role of educating in faith and for faith by parents and the church.

The role of the faith community in nurturing and educating for a life of faith has been a major theme of religious educators for the last thirty years. Writing in 1967, C. Ellis Nelson affirmed the role and place of the congregation in nurturing a life of faith. He said that "faith is communicated by a community of believers and the meaning of faith is developed by its members out of their history, by their interaction with each other, and in relationship to the events that take place in their lives."[13]

Twenty-five years ago, religious educator John Westerhoff asked the question that was the title of his book, "Will our children have faith?" He believed that if the only place where children were intentionally nurtured in faith was the church school, we were in trouble. He went so far as to say that the schooling/instructional model of the church school was bankrupt and should be replaced with a faith-enculturation paradigm. "Both we and our children will have Christian faith if we join with others in a worshipping, learning, witnessing Christian community of faith."[14]

For both Nelson and Westerhoff, to limit learning about faith to a church school classroom was inadequate. The model that they have advocated calls for intentionality and responsibility by the whole congregation in religious education that is, to use the language of Maria Harris, "physical and storied."

Building on the thinking of these two educators, Barbara Kimes Myers and William R. Myers have identified four core conditions that they believe characterize effective Christian ministry with children. Myers and Myers have identified these conditions for the context of ministry with young children in a congregation. As you think about these concepts, consider their implication for other age groups in the church and their application in the home. An effective and "good" ministry with young children open to intentional "education" occurs when adults are (1) caring presences capable of (2) providing hospitality in which (3) the children's contextual experience is honored and in which (4) transcendence is expected.[15]

For my friends Barbara and Bill Myers, a congregation is in ministry with children when it is present with children, welcoming them to a life of faith by providing hospitality and encouraging their gifts of leadership in the church and in the world. A congregation lives out its baptismal promises when it honors and values the experiences of children, their particular angle of vision on the world. The last core condition is an attitude of expectancy and hope. To transcend is "to climb over." "The word transcendence points at the process of moving over, going beyond, across, or through real or imagined limits, obstacles, or boundaries."[16]

I was engaged in consulting with members of a congregation about their settings and topics for adult religious education. It had been a stimulating weekend as we explored together subjects and formats that challenged and supported adults in formal settings for teaching and learning in the church. Worship on the Sunday I was there celebrated Children's Sabbath.[17] I had no idea what awaited me in the worship service.

The prelude, "Jesus Loves Me," was followed by the introit sung by the children's choir. The time of gathering in prayer included thanksgiving for the congregation's participation with a nearby day care center and for all child care providers. The Gospel lesson was told by four storytellers, children in simple costumes, who acted out the parable of the widow and the unjust judge (Luke 18:1–8). The prayer after the offering was given by a child who concluded her words with the confession, "I'm sorry we ate the apple." During the last hymn, musical instruments appeared across the front of the sanctuary, and children left their seats in the congregation and took their places with the instruments, leading us in the response to the blessing as we sang together "Go Now in Peace."[18]

Caring adults spent time rehearsing with children. A congregation has made a commitment to these children and to the children in the neighborhood to be hospitable and welcoming to them—their health, their safety, and their spiritual growth, in both the dailiness and the holiness of life. The leadership of children in worship, their particular gifts and abilities that grow out of their life experiences, was affirmed. And in this worship, transcendence happened. It happened for me at many moments in watching children sing, in hearing the Gospel as they told it through words and actions. It was told, not read. A limit of my perception and understanding of offering was expanded in a child's simple statement of confession.

A faithful ecology is supported when we recognize birthmarks and watermarks, the signs and symbols linking us in faith and in community.

BEING FAITHFUL TOGETHER

God has given me the tongue of a teacher,
that I may know how to sustain the weary with a word. (Isa. 50:4)

At different times in our lives, I imagine we have all prayed to God to give us "the tongue of a teacher" so that we might know just the right thing to say or do as we practice the presence of God in our lives. Parents particularly should be given this gift since living

with children presents minute-by-minute opportunities for learning and growing in faith.

I first became convinced of the importance of a faith ecology
many years ago when I was working as an educational consultant
with three Presbyterian churches. I offered a workshop for parents
to talk together about worship in the home and some things parents could do with their children that would support what we were
offering at church. I began by talking about the idea of simple
worship experiences in the home, and someone asked jokingly,
"Do we have to have a sermon and take up an offering?" At that
moment, I knew there was an opportunity for teaching and learning about what is worship, the elements of worship, and what
might be included in brief experiences of worship in the home.

As I move in and out of congregations in various places in the
country, I meet and hear from adults who are committed to their
own spiritual growth as well as that of their children. They have
made a commitment to the practice of being in worship, learning
with other adults, or teaching in church settings. Practicing their
faith in ministry settings such as shelters, food banks, or mission
projects in the community is a necessary part of their lives. When
it comes to practices at home, many do a great job with blessings
at meals, putting up a nativity scene during Advent and Christmas,
dyeing eggs at Easter, and sometimes helping children make connections with life, death, and resurrection. But there is a lot in between blessings, Advent, and Lent. Three practices are essential in
making a home for faith: rituals of faith, worship with the liturgical year, and connecting the daily with sabbath.

RITUALS OF FAITH

Rituals of faith include acts that help us connect with God, activities or practices that nurture our growing in the life of the
Christian faith. Faithful Jews welcome their Sabbath with the appropriate rituals at the evening meal—lighting candles, saying
prayers, sharing bread and wine from a kiddush cup, greeting each
other in God's name. The ritual binds a family together in faith.

So what binds a Christian family together in faith? Here are
some suggestions for rituals that can grow with your family.
Though this book has a primary focus on a family with young
children, it's also important to think about family practices of faith

that grow with the children as they age. Simple rituals begun with small children may continue to be important even with adolescents. We never know how and in what ways the seeds of faith that we plant may grow, mature, and blossom.

Table Blessings—Repeated, Created, and Sung

There are books of blessings for children and for adults. The blessings that kids learn at camp and come home singing become part of the repertoire of the family. The Johnny Appleseed blessing, "Oh, the Lord is good to me . . . ," probably had its origin at summer camp. The traditional "God Is Great" can be said or sung.

Having a variety of blessings that grow with the ages of the children is important. Holding hands around the table while saying or singing a blessing can be learned by toddlers who watch and listen to those around them. The third kind of blessing is spontaneous, created by the participants. Perhaps a meal on Sunday could be the day when everyone contributes to a "thank you" prayer at the table.

As kids grow older, each family member could take a turn in offering a table blessing of his or her creation. Everyone's participation in this ritual helps children learn that talking with God is not a matter of using big words but relates to having a thankful heart. Children learn to pray by being given opportunities to express their own thoughts with God.

Telling and/or Reading Bible Stories

One way for children and parents to grow together in their knowledge and understanding of the Bible is to read the Bible or a Bible storybook together. A good choice to start is the particular text or story being used in a child's church school class. Reading the text during the week after it has been taught can strengthen the connections between church and home.

If your minister uses the common lectionary for biblical texts each Sunday, you could select one or two of those texts to read during the week prior to Sunday. If you have read the reading from the Hebrew and Christian Scriptures, the psalm, and the epistle or letter, then hearing the texts on Sunday will be like meeting old friends. Don't forget the richness of imagery in the psalms, which children can easily understand.

Bedtime Rituals—Books, Poems, and Prayers

A favorite bedtime ritual for one of my younger nephews is reading books together. He goes to bed earlier than his brothers, and when I'm there, we have wonderful quiet moments just before sleep comes. Christopher snuggles in very close as we read some funny children's books together. Then he has two books he saves for last, stories of Christmas and Easter written by the wonderful children's author Brian Wildsmith. I was reading to Christopher during Lent one evening, and he decided we would read only *The Easter Story,* since we had heard the story about Christmas many times over the last two months, as he reminded me. *The Easter Story* tells what happened between the entry into Jerusalem and concludes with Jesus' ascension. On each page an angel is pictured, and on several pages, there are multitudes of angels, "heavenly hosts" as the Bible says. One of those pages crowded with angels includes the crucifixion of Jesus and the two thieves. Looking at that page with my nephew has given me a new angle of vision for thinking about this horrible moment in the life of Jesus. As we read the page and looked at the pictures together, Christopher said, "Only Jesus can see the angels."

Reading a children's book—whether a picture book for younger children or a chapter book for older children—is a ritual of presence and comfort for the closing of the day. Praying evening prayers together as a time to reflect on the day and remember loved ones is a great ritual for both a child and her parent. As children's lives get as busily scheduled as those of their parents, time for winding down for listening, reading, and conversation enables relaxation of mind, body, and spirit, so sleep may come.

Prayers—"Thanks! Wow! Gimme! and Oops" and "Don't Forget" or "Please Remember"

Chapter 4 described Gellman and Hartman's catchy titles for four familiar kinds of prayers that are used in public worship and in private moments: thanksgiving, adoration, petition, and confession. Children and adults frequently use another kind of prayer, and that is the prayer of intercession when we pray for someone else. I call them the "Please remember!" or "Don't forget!" prayers.

A parent can help a child learn about prayer with prompts like these: What is something we can thank God for today? Did some-

thing happen today that really surprised you? Sometimes we pray
for things we want to happen. Are you thinking of anything like
that? And sometimes we do things that we know we shouldn't. We
sometimes get in trouble, and we say to God, "Oops, I'm sorry."
And we remember people or even a loved pet when we talk with
God and ask God to take care of that person or pet. Praying these
prayers then helps us listen to prayers in worship and notice when
they are used in different parts of the service.

Seasonal Rituals—Planting, Watching, Tending, and Harvesting

Being attuned to nature provides moments for connecting faith
and life. I live in the city surrounded by a lot of tall buildings.
Seeing the western sky is not easy. Sometimes a friend calls me just
at sunset and always makes sure to describe the colors of the sky
and the depth of the hues present in the fading sun of the day. It's
difficult not to say, "Thank you, God," when looking at a beautiful sunset.

After my grandmother died, two good friends of my sister
called and told her they wanted to give her a dogwood tree in
memory of our grandmother. It was her favorite tree. So on an
early fall day, we gathered in the backyard for the planting of the
tree. Each family member shared a story of something he or she remembered that Tat loved. The tree was planted and watered with
careful hands of love and memory and will be a seasonal reminder
of this woman of faith.

Though most of us don't live on farms anymore, we are still
attuned to the rhythms of nature that connect us to a growing understanding of the work of God in this world as Creator and our
responsibility as God's creation in taking care of God's world.
Some activities related to seasonal rituals of the cycles of nature include starting seeds indoors during Lent so that they can be trans-
planted to a garden or a window box outside; celebrating Earth
Day or May Day with a family cleanup project in the yard, around
your apartment building, or somewhere in the neighborhood; and
working in a garden together in your yard, neighborhood, or
church. If there are elderly neighbors or church members who
need help with outside chores, you could have a family work day
to help them in the spring and fall.

Connecting Rituals—Rituals that Connect the
Understanding and Living of the Christian Faith

Many things that happen on a daily basis are opportunities for adults to help a child make connections between faith and life. Conversations about God's work as Creator visible in the natural cycles of beginning of life, living and growing, and death and endings are one concrete way of connection.

The life of a family is very busy. The week is filled with daily rituals of doing homework, participating in after-school activities, preparing meals, cleaning, washing and drying clothes, and caring for pets. The rituals required to keep life going require a lot of time and energy. What is left over for anything extra that explicitly helps us connect what we believe with how we live?

Daily rituals have the potential for connecting us with the ground of our being, our faith and life with God. Preparing and sharing meals connect us to the table at Eucharist. Sharing meals with friends is a ritual of faith.

In the busyness of life, we may find it difficult to think about adding one more thing. Yet an ongoing connection with a ministry or mission of the church may be preparing a meal for someone, hosting an evening in a homeless shelter, volunteering at a church preschool or your child's school to read to children, visiting with people who are unable to leave their homes or elderly members of the church just once a month. When such an activity includes children, they learn about sharing their lives and their gifts with others.

Rituals of Story and Loss

There are times in the life of a family when difficult and painful losses occur. The death of a loved one is grieved by family members, each in their own way. Whether the loss is expected or unexpected, and whether it is a person or a beloved pet, the loss is felt deeply by family members. Such times offer opportunities to remember, to tell stories, and to grieve the loss of one who has been loved and cherished.

Memorial services for family members offer ways for youth and adults to be held faithfully in God's hands within a community of love. Children need rituals to help them move through the steps of loss and grief. Sometimes a family ritual helps on these occasions.

In the summer of 1998, my family gathered to remember the life and faith of my grandmother. At the graveside service, my nephew, Russell, who was seven, read my grandmother's favorite psalm, Psalm 121, which I knew I would not be able to get through myself. Later, as we began to clean out her apartment, her great-grandsons each found something they wanted to keep, and we told stories about "Tat" and remembered her life and her love of her family. In the month before her death, we knew that her life with us was moving toward an end and we had begun to prepare ourselves for that time.

In the summer of 1999, my sister called me with the news that Dobie, one of their Jack Russell terriers, had been hit by a car and died. She and my three nephews had taken the dog to the vet but he didn't make it. This was not a loss for which they were prepared. In talking together through their tears, the children decided they wanted to bury Dobie underneath the tree planted in memory of their grandmother. So we gathered together the day after he died for a ritual of story and memory. My brother-in-law, Lou, had buried Dobie and had left some room for my nephews to add several of his favorite toys. We imagined Dobie in heaven with "Tat," sitting in her lap.

A simple Ritual for a Loved One is appropriate at those times when a family wants and needs to share their grief and loss together. We used this one.

1. Have a prayer: "Thank you, God, for the life of . . ."
2. Ten good things. Each person can contribute something they want to remember about the loved one. [The idea of ten things comes from Judith Viorst, The Tenth Good Thing about Barney (Atheneum, 1971).]
3. Read a psalm, such as part of Psalm 104 (nature and animals), or another biblical selection that is meaningful for the family.
4. Sing a song or hymn that is known to everyone.
5. Blessing. Conclude with a simple blessing: "God bless [name] and all those who loved her/him."
6. Hugs and kisses for everyone!

Rituals Particular to Your Family—Traveling Rituals, Blessings for Goings and Comings

When our family grew from two to four children, taking a family vacation in the summer became a challenge. Six people and a dog in a station wagon became a bit close after the first hundred miles. But we always looked forward to stopping for lunch at the "tail-gate café" as we called it. We found a rest stop, opened up the back of the station wagon, and pulled out the picnic lunch supplies. It became a tradition in our family, a vacation ritual.

We all have rituals in our lives, some explicit, some more implicit. Some parents have a blessing with which they send a child off to school each day. A father waits with his son for the bus to come. It is said that when Elie Wiesel, the author and Holocaust survivor, came home from school each day, his mother asked him, "Have you had a good question today?" Do you have a ritual on Sunday for conversation about church school and worship?

The culture in which we live values quickness, a driving pace of life, and immediate response to needs. Where and when do we stop to pause, to reflect, and to connect faith and life? A ritual that could become important in the life of a family committed to making a home for faith focuses on leisure or vacation time. Many churches have stopped offering church school during some or all of the summer months because so many families are gone on weekends. Attendance at church becomes much more sporadic.

If we believe that growing in the life of the Christian faith is truly a partnership between the home and the congregation, then a way to affirm that relationship is to help parents be good faith educators at the times when the family is away on a weekend. What if churches prepared "sabbath bags" that families could check out to take with them on a vacation or weekend away? The bags could be made out of canvas or cloth and contain materials or items appropriate for different age groups. Bags could be made for preschool children or elementary age children, or bags could be prepared with resources for both age groups. Here are items to include in the bag:

- A copy of *The Family Story Bible* by Ralph Milton.
- A set of children's worship bulletins such as the *Peace Papers*, available from Parenting for Peace and Justice Network. These papers follow the church year and the common lectionary texts and include activities for children and a family page of resources to be read by adults and by children (available by calling 314-533-4445 or by sending E-mail to ppjn@aol.com).

- A Bible storybook related to one of the biblical texts or a children's book from the church library.

- A bibliography of children's books that relate to themes of the biblical texts. Parents could use the bibliography to find the books at the public library or church library.

- A small guide for discussion or art activities to do with children related to the biblical story. Also include a list of art supplies needed for the activities. During family times spent outdoors, an appropriate biblical story is creation and the work of God as Creator.

Families who try this activity might gather together in the fall and share in conversation about how this worked and get responses from the children to observing sabbath while they are away from home and church.

WORSHIP WITH THE LITURGICAL YEAR

A way of making a home for faith is being intentional with *rituals of faith related to the liturgical year.* In their book *Celebrating at Home: Prayers and Liturgies for Families,* Debbie Payden and Laura Loving have reminded us how the church year provides a "framework for understanding who we are as a community of believers. There is a rhythm and rhyme to the yearly flow of church seasons. They walk us through the life and ministry of Jesus Christ, and call us to discipleship in today's world."[19] The seasons of the church year provide a framework for us to move through the story of the Christian faith as we learn and worship at church. Celebrating the seasons of the church year at home helps children make connections between beliefs and actions.

The seasons of the liturgical year are described here with activities for celebration in the home. Also included with each season is a suggestion for connecting the season with an action or expression outside the home.

Advent, Christmas, Epiphany

Advent includes the four Sundays and weeks before Christmas and focuses on waiting and preparation for the birth of the Christchild. In many homes, the bringing out of a nativity or crèche is a family ritual marking the season of Advent. For some families, pieces of the nativity scene are added each week in Advent, saving the placing of the Christchild in the manger for Christmas Eve and the Magi for Epiphany, the twelfth night after Christmas.

When I was a child, our family had a beloved cardboard nativity scene that was always the first thing we looked for when the decorations for our home were unpacked each December. Over the years it became very worn and tattered but still was lovingly displayed. Playing with the pieces of the scene was my way of remembering and retelling the story of the birth of Jesus.

This season of the church year oftentimes gets lost in the mass marketing of Christmas, which begins with the first appearance of home decorations in the stores in October. *Turn Off the Christmas Machine* is the title of a very practical book written to help sensible adults reclaim the meaning of the season. The culture would have us believe the season is about buying, finding the perfect gift, giving, and getting more and more. Advent, I believe, is about slowing down the pace, thoughtful preparing, and making space for hearing again the story of God's greatest gift.

Lighting the Advent candles in worship to mark the four Sundays of the season is a liturgical ritual practiced in many congregations today. This same ritual can be done at home. Since this time of year seems to get busier and more frenetic, planning a simple meal of soup and bread on Sunday evenings that begins with the lighting of the Advent candle and a prayer is a nice way to connect with this season of preparation and waiting. Inviting other families or individuals from church to share in this Sunday ritual is a good way to support one another. Perhaps the meal could be like "stone soup" in the children's story with each person bringing something to add to the soup pot.

Epiphany marks the twelfth night after Christmas and is a day in the church season that is not as well known or observed in the church as are Advent and Christmas. Light is a vivid symbol, reminding us of the star that the Magi followed to find the stable where Jesus was born. Celebrating Epiphany helps Christians remember and live out the fullness of this season of the church year, which begins with Advent. Two activities may mark this day.

Baking a Magi cake is a very old tradition that celebrates this day. It involves hiding small toys such as crowns or rings in the cake batter. After sharing an Epiphany meal with friends, cutting into the cake brings surprises when the lucky ones find the gifts baked inside their slices. Reading the story of the visit of the Magi and placing the figures in the nativity scene are explicit ways of helping children make connection with the story and the surprise that awaited the Magi who had traveled great distances to visit the baby Jesus.

Another concrete experience is to celebrate the season by sharing time and presence with homeless persons or those who are eating in shelters, or elderly or disabled persons who long for conversation and touch with others. Often these people are remembered before Christmas. Why not have a family commitment to gift giving that extends over the whole season of Advent, Christmas, and Epiphany? The gifts of time, conversation, and presence are sometimes more important than brightly wrapped packages.

Season of Lent—Shrove Tuesday, Ash Wednesday, Holy Week

This season has strong cultural as well as religious roots in communities. Carnival in Rio de Janeiro and Mardi Gras in New Orleans are times of lavish parties and celebrations leading up to Shrove Tuesday, the day before the beginning of Lent, which marks a six-week period of reflection prior to Easter. Some faith traditions honor a practice of fasting or giving up something during the season of Lent as a way of emphasizing penitence. The last days of Lent are called Holy Week and often include worship marking Maundy Thursday, Good Friday, the Easter Vigil on Saturday evening, and the celebration of the risen Christ on Easter.

Cultural, familial, and religious traditions are mixed together at Easter as we talk about a cross and an empty tomb, Easter baskets, bunnies and dyed eggs, and the renewing of the earth in spring. Walking through this liturgical season with intention and planning provides a way to remember the meaning behind the day.

Like Advent, Lent is a short season in the liturgical calendar and is appropriate for trying something together as a family, such as telling or reading the stories of Jesus' life. Making a family commitment to learn the Prayer of Jesus or the Apostles' Creed is another activity to do together during Lent.

Depending upon the calendar, Lent begins in February or early March. It often coincides with the beginning of spring sports activities for children and their week of spring break from school. How in the busy lives of working parents and the activities of school-age children do you make time and a priority for activities outside the home that connect the meaning of Lent with our lives in the world?

When I think of the transition from Shrove Tuesday to Ash Wednesday, I am reminded of the movement from excess and abundance to conscious simplicity. Remembering the teachings and the life of Jesus during Lent—the call to lead a simpler life, share wealth and resources, care for others—is still our call today. During this six-week period, families could talk about some of these activities and select one or more to practice during Lent: eat a meal of soup and bread once a week and contribute the money saved to a hunger program in the community;[20] volunteer as a family to serve a meal at a homeless shelter or deliver a meal for elderly or disabled persons once a week during Lent; plant seeds in a small pot of soil to watch them grow and plant them outdoors in the spring; turn off the TV on Sundays and spend time together as a family.

Easter

If there is one holiday other than Christmas that is known and observed by a majority of Christians in the world, it is Easter. Worship services swell with crowds of people, many of whom will not return until the following Christmas or Easter. Mixed in with cultural Christians are the faithful who have marked the journey to Easter through Lent and Holy Week.

For children, an Easter basket with candy, dyed eggs, and a stuffed animal or small toy has become a traditional celebration of this season of the year. I love the creativity and mess involved in dyeing eggs and talking about the symbolism of birth, life, and death represented in eggs. Perhaps the activity of dyeing and decorating eggs could include inviting a few friends from church to join in the fun. Since so many families live apart from grandparents or other relatives, inviting older friends from the congregation for an egg-decorating party would be a way for children to interact with older persons.

Preparing a festive brunch, lunch, or dinner on Easter Sunday is a practice of some families. During the years I lived in Alabama, I was a regular guest in the Beck home for their Easter lunch after church. Their family table always included a variety of friends from church who did not have family living near them. Each place at the table was marked with a decorated egg. Children, young people, and adults shared in the familiar greeting, "Christ is risen, Christ is risen indeed," which moved with us from church to home as we remembered and celebrated the saving work of the risen Christ.

Pentecost

I love this particular day in the liturgical calendar, which comes seven weeks after Easter. It marks the giving of God's Spirit and the beginning of what we know as the church. The red color of fire vividly calls to mind the flames of the spirit of Pentecost. On Pentecost we are reminded that "we are the church together" and that together we possess many varied gifts of God's Spirit (1 Cor. 12:4).

Some activities in the home that help children remember and understand Pentecost include these: tell stories about the church where you attend and how you came to find it and what you like about it; recall the day of your child's baptism and what happened on that special day (look at pictures together if they are available); invite an older member of the church for a Sunday meal and share stories that tell some of the history of the church; if you have a teenager who has been confirmed on Pentecost Sunday, have a special dinner to mark the occasion, inviting family and friends of the confirmand.

Common Time

Common time is the longest season of the church year, beginning with the Sunday after Pentecost and concluding with Christ the King Sunday, which is the last Sunday before the beginning of Advent in November or December. Three religious/cultural days are important in this season: World Communion Sunday, All Saints' Day, and Thanksgiving. They focus on honoring the past, affirming the present, and looking to the future with faithful memory and hope.

World Communion Sunday offers families the opportunity to think about Christians all over the world coming to the table of Jesus Christ. Baking bread together or sampling bread of other cultures (pita, tortillas, rice cakes) is a visible way of connecting the bread we eat with the bread that helps us remember Jesus and our living in the world.

On All Saints' Day, congregations and families name the saints who have gone before us. Recalling the names of church members and family members who have died and telling stories of their lives help us remember the continuing story of God's people. Making a family tree on paper with leaves to add for the names of family members is a visual way to teach children about their history.

A Thanksgiving meal is an ideal time for simple expressions of thanksgiving by each person at the table: "Today, I thank God for . . ." Opening your Thanksgiving table to someone who might not have family or friends with whom to share a meal is a way of saying thanks to God for food and family.

CONNECTING THE DAILY WITH SABBATH

Finally, there are ways of honoring *sabbath* and connecting it with our lives during the rest of the week. "Sabbath is the reminder that presence is God's way of being in our midst, our way of being with God, and the way in which we are with one another. . . . In sabbath we try to become attuned to holiness in time."[21]

When I was a child growing up in the South, we dressed up on Sunday to go to church. My grandmother made sure I had plenty of white cotton gloves to wear with my Sunday dresses. I look back at some of those Easter Sunday pictures and compare them with collages of children today. There is a great deal more diversity in practices today than when I was a child in the 1950s. For some congregations, dressing for Sunday is still a norm across the ages. For others, men in coats and ties and women in "Sunday dresses" are typical only among the older generation. For some African American congregations, dressing in traditional African clothing or wearing shirts or dresses made from African cloth is becoming a norm for dressing up and a way of remembering and honoring cultural heritage. In many churches today, the norm for children to wear "church clothes" has disappeared, and the clothes for Sunday are often the same as those worn to school. So what makes Sunday different?

As a child, I knew Sunday was different because the rhythms of the day were different, I wore different clothing, and I went to church with my family. It was a day to spend with family at home and at church. Growing up in the fifties in the South meant there was nothing else competing for our attention—no soccer games, gymnastics competition, shopping, or twenty-five channels of sports on television.

The challenge of sabbath in our culture is one of making priorities. Sunday as a culturally protected religious day is no longer a reality for Christians. As the cartoon character Pogo said, "We have met the enemy and he is us." The honoring of sabbath is no longer legislated by blue laws, protected by community recreation norms, or visibly acknowledged by the finery of our clothing. The honoring of sabbath becomes a matter of individual and familial vocation. We choose how we make our Sundays sabbath and how to connect sabbath with the rest of the week. We choose from among many, many options.

Some ways of honoring sabbath include these ideas:

- Light a Christ candle. Place a white pillar candle on the dining table. Light the candle on Sundays as a way of marking a day set aside for rest, reflection, worship, and learning with a faith community.

- During the week, read one of the lectionary texts or scriptures used in church school or worship.

- Bake and/or share bread on Sundays when there is communion. Bake two loaves, and share one with a stranger or friend.

- Practice the prayers or responses (spoken and sung) used in worship.

- Be intentional about spending time together as family and sharing family times with others.

PARTNERING IN FAITH: WHAT DOES GOD REQUIRE OF YOU?

Maria Harris defines spirituality as "our way of being in the world in light of the Mystery at the core of the universe; a mystery that some of us call God. The term also includes understanding what that Mystery requires of us, such as the classic set of demands recorded in Micah 6:8: 'to do justice, and to love kindness, and to walk humbly with your God.'"[22]

Through the love and care of parents, family, and friends at home and nursery workers and preschool teachers at church, school, or day care, children come to experience the world and people as trusting. There is no greater tool of evangelism for a church than to have bright, clean, and hospitable nurseries and preschool classes, staffed by caring and loving teachers. The difficult separation from a parent is made easier for a child when there are other loving arms to hold her. The first experiences of children and parents in congregational settings matter. They quickly learn if children are valued, if they are important in the life of the congregation, if there is a priority for their presence and contribution to its life, work, mission, and ministry.

In teaching young people and adults about their role as teachers or caregivers in the church nursery, I emphasize three ways a child first begins to know God, to experience faith, and to learn about church. These are goals for a child's growth in the life of the Christian faith. All children should be able to learn and know that (1) the church is a welcoming place where teachers and the congregational context contribute to a warm, safe, caring, and happy environment; (2) there are people in addition to their parents and family who love them, who are glad to interact with them; they have a second family where they can be at home, the church; and (3) there is a special book that tells us about God, the Bible.

Westerhoff believes that by the time a child begins kindergarten or first grade, she or he learns about faith through affiliation, through participating in a congregation and its story, its tradition, its living of the faith: "We depend on significant others for the stories that explain our lives and how our people live. Belonging to a community is very important in order to fulfill our need to be wanted and accepted."[23]

In what ways does your congregation provide affiliative experiences for its children, ways that they can visibly learn about doing justice, loving kindness, and humbly walking? Consider this list:

Children are included at coffee and juice time between or after worship services.

Children are welcomed and included in worship. Children's bulletins are available.[24]

Children are present for the sacraments of baptism and Eucharist. References to the experiences of children and young

people as well as the experiences of adults are made in sermons.
During the prayers of the people, concerns of children are welcomed and included.

Opportunities for expressing faith through mission or service
projects are available to groups across the ages.

Children's participation in stewardship education and learning
about sharing money, time, and talents are encouraged.

The leadership of children and young people as ushers, liturgists,
and musicians is encouraged.

Space for children to play is available. Booster seats are available
for use in the sanctuary and for church meals (as well as high
chairs for meals).

Ministers have time for conversations with children and young
people and call them by name.

Children with special needs (physical, mental, or emotional) are
welcomed and included.

Adults in the congregation invite children and young people into
their lives through conversation, companionship, and working
and serving together.

The many ways that children (and all of us) learn are valued and
encouraged: hearing, seeing, touching, movement, reasoning, and
through musical, artistic, and dramatic expression.[25]

A HOME FOR FAITH

Zacchaeus must have been surprised by Jesus' call to him. All he
had wanted to do was to see the man whom everyone was talking about. Hosting him in his home was probably not what
Zacchaeus had imagined would take place. He quickly climbed
down from the tree and found himself looking into Jesus' face of
faith. Jesus' questions and expectations were difficult. But
Zacchaeus knew what he must do to live a different kind of life,
one that was consistent when he was at home and when he was
away from home.

A faithful ecology requires this connection and commitment to
love God and our neighbor. The earliest experiences of living into
this lifestyle begin with the commitment of families to making a
home for faith.

QUESTIONS FOR REFLECTION AND DISCUSSION

1. When you were a child, what was your family's tradition of table blessings?

2. How were the liturgical seasons of the year celebrated in your home as a child? What seasonal traditions are important in your family today?

3. Read the suggestions with regard to rituals. Which of these are ones you are already doing? Which are ones you would like to try? What are some new ideas that emerge in conversation with other parents?

   If you're discussing this chapter with a small group, here are some additional questions you might use:

4. Recall the Myerses' four core conditions for ministry with children: the presence of caring people who provide hospitality, while honoring the experience of each child; and in the process of this kind of ministry, transcendence is expected. Where are these conditions in evidence in your congregation?

5. Share the spoken or sung blessings you like to use at mealtime with your family.

6. What do you think about the idea of vacation or "sabbath bags" to take with you when you're out of town on a weekend in the summer? What things would you like to see in the bag?

7. As parents, what kind of assistance would you like from the church in supporting your role as faith educators in helping your child grow in the life of the Christian faith? What can the church expect from you?

8. Use this open-ended sentence to close a time together: As a parent and as Christian, I am called to . . .

6

WHERE DO I GO FOR MORE HELP?

Fortunately, we live in a time in which resources abound for helping our children learn about God and think about what faith means in their lives. The difficulty comes in determining criteria for selection because of the wealth and variety of books that are available. Bookstores in your city or town, whether they are large chains such as Barnes & Noble or Cokesbury or independently owned ones, often have extensive sections on religion and faith.

Equally accessible are books that can be ordered from denominational publishing houses such as The Pilgrim Press/United Church Press (1-800-537-3394). Shopping for books on the Web at sources such as Amazon.com means that resources are only one click away.

This last chapter is bibliographic, providing sources for books for church libraries or resource centers and for personal libraries at home. Also suggested here is a beginning list of Web sites for church professionals and for laypeople interested in connecting with biblical resources available for computers and use in educational settings at church and at home. Since space is limited, consider this a beginning point for your resource list.

PRINT RESOURCES

Books for parents or family members who are interested in nurturing a child's faith can be divided into several categories. It would be useful to have all of these books available in a church resource center.

- "Help! I don't know what to do and I need a quick answer for my child!"

Marc Gellman and Thomas Hartman. *Where Does God Live? Questions and Answers for Parents and Children.* Triumph Books, 1987.

———. *How Do You Spell God? Answers to the Big Questions from Around the World.* Morrow Junior Books, 1995.

———. *Lost and Found: A Kid's Book for Living Through Loss.* Morrow Junior Books, 1999. Written for eight- to twelve-year-olds, this book deals with loss of a friend, a game, health, divorce, trust, confidence, and losing because of death.

David Heller. *Talking to Your Child about God: A Book for Families of All Faiths.* Bantam, 1988.

Harold Kushner. *When Children Ask about God: A Guide for Parents Who Don't Always Have All the Answers.* Schocken Books, 1989.

- "I need a book I can read through slowly that helps me as a parent who is also interested in growing in faith along with my child."

Polly Berrien Berends. *Gently Lead: How to Teach Your Children about God While Finding Out for Yourself.* Harper, 1991.

Betty Shannon Cloyd. *Children and Prayer: A Shared Pilgrimage.* Upper Room Books, 1997.

Jean Grasso Fitzpatrick. *Something More: Nurturing Your Child's Spiritual Growth.* Viking, 1991.

- "I just want something to read for my daily meditation or devotion."

Alive Now, a devotional magazine available for $11.95 for a one-year subscription from P.O. Box 37142, Boone IA 50037-2142.

The Book of Daily Prayer. United Church Press, annual. This collection of morning and evening prayers follows the common lectionary texts.

Marian Wright Edelman. *Guide My Feet: Prayers and Meditations for Our Children.* Harper, 1995.

Holding Children in Prayer: A Lenten Guide. The Children's Defense Fund, 1997.

Martin Marty and Micah Marty have a series of books published by Eerdmans that contain reflection on biblical texts and photographs designed for meditation. They include *When True Simplicity Is Gained*, 1998; *The Promise of Winter*, 1997; *Places along the Way*, 1995; and *Our Hope for Years to Come*, 1994.

Ann Weems. *Kneeling in Bethlehem*. Westminster/John Knox, 1980.

———. *Kneeling in Jerusalem*. Westminster/John Knox, 1992.

- "What are some resources I can read with my child to explain about loss or death?"

Marc Gellman and Thomas Hartman. *Lost and Found: A Kid's Book for Living Through Loss*. Morrow Junior Books, 1999.

Sharon Greenlee. *When Someone Dies*. Peachtree Publishers, 1992.

Bryan Mellonie and Robert Ingpen. *Lifetimes: The Beautiful Way to Explain Death to Children*. Bantam, 1983.

Doris Sanford. *It Must Hurt a Lot: A Child's Book about Death*. Multnomah Press, 1986.

- "We want some resources to help us think about family activities related to faith."

Martha Bettis Gee. *Things to Make and Do for Advent and Christmas, Things to Make and Do for Lent and Easter,* and *Things to Make and Do for Pentecost*. Bridge Resources, Presbyterian Church, USA, 1997.

Nancy Luenn. *Celebrations of Light: A Year of Holidays around the World*. Atheneum Books for Young Children, 1998.

Deborah Alberswerth Payden and Laura Loving. *Celebrating at Home: Prayers and Liturgies for Families*. United Church Press, 1998.

Holly W. Whitcomb. *Feasting with God: Adventures in Table Spirituality*. United Church Press, 1996.

There are two excellent magazines available for children and young people. *Pockets* has stories and activities designed for children ages six through twelve; a one-year subscription costs $16.95. *Devo'Zine* is a devotional magazine for young people; a one-year subscription costs $16.95. Both are available from P.O. Box 856, Nashville, TN 37202-9719.

- "Our church wants to offer a class or small group for parents related to their role as faith educators with their children. What are some good books or resources we might look at together?"

Marc Gellman. *God's Mailbox: More Stories about Stories in the Bible.* Morrow Junior Books, 1996.

Marc Gellman and Oscar de Mejo. *Does God Have a Big Toe? Stories about Stories in the Bible.* Harper, 1989.

Growing Together, a series of 24- to 32-page books for parents and adults interested in nurturing children in the life of the Christian faith. These are published by the United Church Press (1-800-537-3394). Titles available include *Talking with Your Child about Aids; Talking with Your Child about the Bible; Talking with Your Child about Change; Talking with Your Child about the Church Year; Talking with Your Child about Fantasy and Dreams; Talking with Your Child about Feelings; Talking with Your Child about God's Story; Talking with Your Child about Prayer; Talking with Your Child about the Presence of God; Talking with Your Child about Sexuality; Talking with Your Child about Worship.*

Maria Harris. *The Faith of Parents.* Paulist Press, 1991.

Deborah Alberswerth Payden and Laura Loving. *Celebrating at Home: Prayers and Liturgies for Families.* United Church Press, 1998.

Marjorie J. Thompson. *Family, the Form Center: A Vision of the Role of Family in Spiritual Formation.* Upper Room Books, 1996.

John Westerhoff. *Bringing Up Children in the Christian Faith.* HarperSanFrancisco, 1980.

There is a set of three booklets available for use with parents. Carol Wehrheim wrote *The Journey Ahead: A Bible Study for Expectant Parents,* which includes suggestions for using the study in a small group. *Beginning a Journey* by Betty McLaney makes a great gift for parents bringing their child to church for baptism or dedication. *Step by Step* is a first-year calendar designed to be used by parents as they move through this important time in the life of their child. All three books are available from the Presbyterian Publishing House, Louisville, Kentucky.

- "As pastor or educator, what books should I be reading as background for leading a conversation with a group of parents interested in making a home for faith?"

Elizabeth F. Caldwell. *Come Unto Me: Rethinking the Sacraments for Children.* United Church Press, 1996.

Sofia Cavalletti. *The Religious Potential of the Child.* Liturgy Training Publications, 1992.

Robert Coles. *The Spiritual Life of Children.* Houghton Mifflin, 1990.

Marc Gellman and Thomas Hartman. *How Do You Spell God? Answers to the Big Questions from Around the World.* Morrow Junior Books, 1995.

———. *Lost and Found: A Kid's Book for Living Through Loss.* Morrow Junior Books, 1999. Written for eight- to twelve-year-olds, this book deals with loss of a friend, a game, health, divorce, trust, confidence, and losing because of death.

Barbara Kimes Myers. *Young Children and Spirituality.* Routledge, 1997.

William R. Myers and Barbara Kimes Myers. *Engaging in Transcendence: The Church's Ministry and Covenant with Young Children.* Pilgrim Press, 1992.

Mary Pipher. *The Shelter of Each Other: Rebuilding Our Families.* Grosset/Putnam, 1996.

BOOKS FOR CHILDREN
Preschool-Age Children

Kathleen Long Bostrom and Peter Adderley. *The World That God Made.* Tyndale for Kids, 1997. Kathy is doing a series titled Questions for Little Hearts. The first two books in the series are *What Is God Like?*, 1998, and *Who Is Jesus?*, 1999 ($9.99 each). Through poetry, children are invited to think about what God is like. This is a great resource for parents because each of the concepts for God with related biblical texts is explained at the back of the book.

Ray Buckley. *God's Love Is Like.* Abingdon, 1998.

Marie-Agnes Gaudrat. *What Is God Like?* Liturgical Press, 1998.

Sheila Hamanaka. *All the Colors of the Earth.* Morrow, 1994.

Carolyn Pogue. *A Creation Story.* ParseNip Press, 1998.

Lois Rock. *Before the Stars Were Made.* Chariot Victor Publishing, 1997.

———. A First Look Series. Includes three books: *A First Look at God, A First Look at Prayer,* and *A First Look at the Bible.* Chariot Victor Publishing, 1997.

———. *The Gentle Carpenter.* Lion Publishing, 1997.

Margaret Spivey. *I Can't Make a Flower.* Judson Press, 1994.

Nancy Sweetland. *God's Quiet Things.* Eerdmans, 1998.

Word and Picture Books. There are eighteen small books in this series. Each page of each book focuses on one word with a simple story line. Titles include *God Is Our Home, Helping Others, Jesus Goes Fishing.* They are available in sets of six from United Church Press (1-800-537-3394).

Children of All Ages

Carolyn Stahl Bohler. *God Is Like a Mother Hen.* Presbyterian Publishing House, 1996.

Ruth Boling, Lauren J. Buzy, and Laurie A. Vance. *A Children's Guide to Worship.* Geneva Press, 1997.

Nancy White Carlstrom. *Does God Know How to Tie Shoes?* Eerdmans, 1993.

Children of America. *The 11th Commandment: Wisdom from Our Children.* Jewish Lights Publishing, 1996.

Robert Coles. *The Story of Ruby Bridges.* Scholastic, 1995.

Jane Cowen-Fletcher. *It Takes a Village.* Scholastic, 1994.

Mary Ann Getty-Sullivan. *God Speaks to Us in Feeding Stories.* Liturgical Press, 1997.

———. *God Speaks to Us in Water Stories.* Liturgical Press, 1997.

———. *God Speaks to Us in Dreams and Visions.* Liturgical Press, 1998.

Paul Goble. *Dream Wolf.* Bradbury, 1990.

Betsy Hearne. *Seven Brave Women.* Greenwillow Books, 1997.

Barbara M. Joosse. *Mama, Do You Love Me?* Chronicle Books, 1991.

Dennis Linn, Sheila Fabricant Linn, and Matthew Linn. *Sleeping with Bread: Holding What Gives You Life.* Paulist Press, 1995.

Barry Lopez. *Crow and Weasel.* A Sunburst Book. Farrar, Straus & Giroux, 1990.

Betsy and Giulio Maestrao. *The Story of Religion.* Clarion Books, 1996. This is a great introduction to the practice of religion by many faith traditions in the world today.

Saviour Pirotta. *Joy to the World: Christmas Stories from Around the Globe.* HarperCollins, 1998.

Patricia Polacco. *The Keeping Quilt.* Simon & Schuster, 1988.

Gail Ramshaw has written a series of books that explain the parts of worship to children. They include *1, 2, 3, Church and Everyday and Sunday, Too* (Augsburg, 1996), and *Sunday Morning* (Liturgy Training Publications, 1993).

Faith Ringgold. *Tar Beach.* Crown Publishers, 1991.

Sylvia Rosa-Casanova. *Mama Provi and the Pot of Rice.* Atheneum, 1997.

Michael J. Rosen. *The Greatest Table.* Harcourt Brace, 1994.

Sandy Eisenberg Sasso. *God's Paintbrush.* Jewish Lights Publishing, 1992.

———. *In God's Name.* Jewish Lights Publishing, 1994.

———. *But God Remembered: Stories of Women from Creation to the Promised Land.* Jewish Lights Publishing, 1995.

———. *God in Between.* Jewish Lights Publishing, 1998.

Nancy Sohn Swartz. *In Our Image: God's First Creatures.* Jewish Lights Publishing, 1998.

Bijou le Tord. *The River and the Rain: The Lord's Prayer.* Doubleday, 1996.

Douglas Wood. *Old Turtle.* Pfeifer-Hamilton, 1992.

BOOKS FOR CHRISTMAS AND EASTER

These books as well as the ones in the next list make great Christmas presents. Giving one at Easter, along with the Easter basket, is a way to celebrate religious and cultural meanings of the holiday.

Peter Collington. *A Small Miracle.* Jonathan Cape, 1997.

Margery Facklam. *Only a Star.* Eerdmans, 1996.

Norma Farber. *When It Snowed That Night.* A Laura Geringer Book. HarperCollins, 1993.

Aileen Fisher. *The Story of Easter.* HarperCollins, 1997.

Mem Fox. *Wombat Divine.* Harcourt Brace, 1995.

Melissa Kajpust. *A Dozen Silk Diapers: A Christmas Story.* Hyperion, 1993.

Patricia Polacco. *Rechenka's Eggs.* Putnam and Grosset, 1988.

Helen Earle Simcos. *For All the World.* Augsburg, 1994.

Julie Vivas, illustrator. *The Nativity.* Harcourt Brace Jovanovich, 1986.

Brian Wildsmith. *A Christmas Story.* Knopf, 1989.

———. *The Easter Story.* Knopf, 1993.

Isabel Wilner. *B Is for Bethlehem: A Christmas Alphabet.* Puffin Unicorn Books, 1990.

Barbara Younger and Lisa Flinn. *One Morning in Joseph's Garden: An Easter Story.* Abingdon, 1998.

CHILDREN'S BIBLES, BIBLE STORYBOOKS

Joan Baro. *The Bible: A People Listen to God.* Liturgical Press, 1995. This book does a good job of telling the whole story of the Bible, covering both the Hebrew Scriptures and the Christian Scriptures.

John Bierhorst. *The Woman Who Fell from the Sky: The Iroquois Story of Creation.* Morrow, 1993.

Tomie De Paola. *Book of Bible Stories.* Putnam, 1990.

———. *Book of the Old Testament.* Putnam, 1995.

———. *Parables of Jesus.* Holiday House, 1995.

———. *Miracles of Jesus.* Holiday House, 1996.

Selina Hastings. *The Children's Illustrated Bible.* D.K. Publishing, 1994.

Madeleine L'Engle. *Ladder of Angels: Stories from the Bible, Illustrated by Children of the World.* Harper, 1979.

Julius Lester. *When the Beginnings Began: Stories about God, the Creatures, and Us.* Harcourt Brace, 1999.

Ella K. Lindvall. *Read Aloud Bible Stories.* Moody Press, vol. 1, 1986; vol. 2, 1987; vol. 3, 1990.

Ralph Milton. *The Family Story Bible.* Presbyterian Publishing House, 1997.

John and Katherine Paterson. *Images of God.* Clarion, 1998. The authors focus on word images that help describe God's presence in the world.

Ruth Sanderson. *Tapestries: Stories of Women in the Bible.* Little, Brown, 1998. Contains stories of Eve, Rebekah, Miriam, Rahab, Deborah, Jael, Ruth, Hannah, Abigail, Bathsheba, the queen of Sheba, and the witch of Endor.

Diane Wolkstein. *Esther's Story.* Morrow Junior Books, 1996.

WORLD WIDE WEB AND OTHER MEDIA RESOURCES

Web sites are fast-growing resources available to churches and families. Here is a very short list of Web sites that have educational resources important for those who would make a home for faith. Links to additional Web sites are available at the home pages of these sites.

Alternatives for Simple Living is an organization committed to offering books and resources for helping families and congregations learn ways to live more simply and justly and to celebrate responsibly.
Phone: 1-800-821-6153
E-mail: AltSimLiv@aol.com
http://www.members.aol.com/AltSimLiv/simple.html

The Children's Defense Fund has a mission to "Leave No Child Behind." It works to ensure that every child has a healthy start, a head start, a fair start, a safe start, and a moral start. It makes available educational and liturgical materials for the celebration of Children's Sabbath in October.
http://www.childrensdefense.org

The Parenting for Peace and Justice Network provides help, advocacy, and education about raising children to be peacemakers in the world. The Web site includes information about the Parenting for Peace and Justice Network and Families Against Violence Advocacy Network.
Phone: 314-533-4445
E-mail: ppjn@aol.com
http://www.members.aol.com/ppjn/index.html

UNICEF's Web address is http://www.unicef.org.

Sunday School Software Ministries provides critical assessment of CD-ROM Bible programs available for purchase in stores. Neil MacQueen, a Presbyterian pastor, has created this invaluable resource for teachers and educators working with curricular material for settings in religious education. Seasonal catalogs can be received through the mail. Links to other Web sites working with educational materials for use with classes in the church school are also available from the Web site.

Phone: 1-800-678-1948

E-mail: Sundaysoft@ee.net

www.sundaysoftware.com

Anyone interested in a comprehensive catalog of video resources for use in teaching should get a copy of the Travarca Catalog from the Reformed Church in America.

Phone: 1-800-968-7221

E-mail: travarca@lserv.net

APPENDIX 1: FAITH STATEMENTS

These faith statements were written by two young women as part of their preparation for confirmation at Lincoln Park Presbyterian Church in Chicago.

FAITH STATEMENT
by Kirsten Stangenes

I had a rough time writing out my faith and I know why. It wasn't because I didn't have any idea why I was committing myself to the teachings of God. It wasn't because my pencil broke. It was because I had to speak for myself to God and God's believers about what I had decided to do and why I was doing it.

Life is not always easy, but then . . . it's not always hard either, especially with the help of God and his son Jesus Christ. God is always looking over us as different persons. It's as if God has a trillion, zillion hearts and eyes and always knows how everyone feels and everyone's view.

Dreams are the most important thing that I depend upon God for. Dreams are for everyone. You can never hope for something too much. God knows what is best and will always give something even though it's not exactly what you had in mind.

Dreams are what make the world go round. Without dreams people would not have anything to look forward to and would feel downright miserable. We all dream of peace, education, happiness, true love, careers, marriage, friendship, adventures, family, animals, nature, vacations, parties.

God gave us a mind, a heart, a soul, a spirit and all necessities for life. Jesus was the example and taught us lessons about how to live.

Where do you capture that self-esteem when you want to speak out and help others?

Where do you get that courage to say goodbye to a loved one when they pass on? Where do you get that confidence to do well in a new job entrusted to you? From God and Jesus, of course.

No matter who you are or what you are, where you come from or where you go, you know you have a friend somewhere.

A spirit of love, a stone-strong soul, joy from the rising golden sun and time is all you need to know that God is with you every step of the way.

STATEMENT OF FAITH
by Allison Denny

I believe in one God, the God of all people. God brings all people of every race and color together. I believe that God sheds new light on everything we do as humans.

I believe in Jesus Christ, the son of God who proclaimed the good news and preached the word of God to all people across the world. Jesus brought all Christians together under the single belief of one great and powerful God.

I believe that the church is a meeting place for people to come together and worship God. The church also serves for many other great purposes. It is a place for people to celebrate their lives together.

All Christians are individuals, and by ourselves we are not whole. But together we are a congregation. The church is like a puzzle—everyone has different talents and qualities, and if one piece was missing we would not be whole.

I believe I can be a faithful member of this church, and a faithful servant for God. Jesus is a guide for all of us to follow. He shows us the way to love and forgive. I can help teach my fellow sisters and brothers of the church.

I support the work of this church, trying to use inclusive language, and accepting gay, lesbian and straight people to this congregation of faith.[1]

Here is a simple form for articulating your Christian beliefs. On the left side of the form are the categories for you to use in thinking about what you believe. In the middle is a place for you to write some words or sentences. What can you say about your understanding of God as Creator, Redeemer, and Spirit? What do you know and believe about the Bible? When you think about the church, what is important to you to affirm? And what are your gifts for ministry in this world as a Christian? What is God calling you to do and to be? The column on the right side gives you a chance to think about how you would interpret your beliefs to your child. Take some time and work on this faith statement.

Here I Stand

	What I Believe	How I Communicate to My Child
God—Creator		
God—Redeemer		
God—Sustainer		
The Bible		
The Church (Worship, Sacraments, Mission)		
My Call as a Christian in the World		

In his book *Story Journey: An Invitation to the Gospel as Storytelling,* Thomas Boomershine uses a variety of stories in the life of Jesus as examples of how we can learn to become storytellers, using the Bible as a source. "The authority of the Scriptures is based on their role as the source of our knowledge of God. Thus, entering into the story journey of the gospel tradition is a pilgrimage to a primary source of the revelation of God in Jesus Christ."[1] Boomershine identifies four steps involved in the process of preparing to tell a biblical story.

1. Learn the story by listening for the structure. As you read a story such as the baptism of Jesus, note the parts or episodes of the story. Where is the emphasis of the writer of the story? Boomershine believes that looking for verbal threads in the story helps with remembering: "Verbal threads are words that are repeated either exactly or with minor variations."[2] As you read a story, notice the verbal threads that help to pull the story together. All of these steps prepare you to begin to learn the story, one episode at a time.

2. Listen to the story. This involves considering the background and details. What additional information about the story in its context is it important for you to find out?

3. Make connections. Boomershine believes that making a link between the biblical story and our personal or communal experiences enables our telling of the story to have both "depth and distinctiveness."[3]

4. Tell the story. It is essential to tell the story in a way appropriate to you. Boomershine emphasizes that the point of telling a Bible story is not performance but the act of giving a gift.

Preface

1. Ronald S. Cole-Turner, "Child of Blessing, Child of Promise," *The Presbyterian Hymnal* (Louisville: Westminster/John Knox Press, 1990).

2. My thanks to Rev. Nancy H. Enderle, who first suggested this title for parents in a paper she wrote while a student at McCormick Theological Seminary.

3. Horace Bushnell, *Christian Nurture* (New York: C. Scribner's Sons, 1888).

1. A Halo, a Star, and a Bathrobe

1. Patrick D. Miller, *Deuteronomy: Interpretation: A Bible Commentary for Teaching and Preaching* (Louisville: Westminster/John Knox Press, 1990), 66.

2. Elizabeth Francis Caldwell, *Come Unto Me: Rethinking the Sacraments for Children* (Cleveland: United Church Press, 1996), 62.

3. The two metaphors, organic and journey, are discussed by Craig Dykstra in *Growing in the Life of Faith: Education and Christian Practices* (Louisville: Geneva Press, 1999), 35.

4. The parable of the sower in Luke 8:4–8 illustrates this metaphor.

5. Dykstra, *Growing in the Life of Faith,* 35.

6. C. Ellis Nelson, *Where Faith Begins* (Louisville: Westminster/John Knox Press, 1967), 10.

7. See Charles Foster, *Educating Congregations: The Future of Christian Education* (Nashville: Abingdon, 1994), and John Westerhoff, *Will Our Children Have Faith?* (New York: Seabury, 1976).

8. Sandy Eisenberg Sasso, *God in Between* (Woodstock, Vt.: Jewish Lights Publishing, 1998).

9. Thanks to Kathleen Norris who used this phrase in her book *Amazing Grace: A Vocabulary of Faith* (New York: Riverhead Books, 1998).

10. Marc Gellman, *God's Mailbox: More Stories about Stories in the Bible* (New York: Morrow Junior Books, 1996), xii, xiii.

11. Nelle Morton, *The Journey Is Home* (Boston: Beacon Press, 1985), xix.

12. Walter Brueggemann, "Confirmation: Joining a Special Story," *Colloquy* (May–June 1974): 9.

13. Sharon Daloz Parks, quoted in Parks, Laurent A. Parks Daloz, Cheryl H. Keen, and James P. Keen, *Common Fire: Lives of Commitment in a Complex World* (Boston: Beacon Press, 1996), 31.

14. Martin Marty, "Christian Education in a Pluralistic Culture," in *Rethinking Christian Education: Explorations in Theory and Practice,* ed. David S. Schuller (St. Louis: Chalice Press, 1993), 22.

15. Ibid., 23.

16. Dorothy Bass, ed., *Practicing Our Faith: A Way of Life for a Searching People* (San Francisco: Jossey-Bass, 1997), 5.

17. Ibid., 200.

18. Parks et al., *Common Fire,* 211.

19. Sharon Daloz Parks, "Home and Pilgrimage: Companion Metaphors for Personal and Social Transformation," *Soundings* 72, nos. 2–3 (summer–fall 1989): 304.

20. Carol Lakey Hess, *Caretakers of Our Common House: Women's Development in Communities of Faith* (Nashville: Abingdon, 1997), 209.

21. Madeleine L'Engle, *A Severed Wasp* (New York: Farrar, Straus & Giroux, 1982), 16.

22. Dwayne Huebner, "Christian Growth in Faith," *Religious Education* 81, no. 4 (fall 1986): 516.

23. Elizabeth F. Caldwell, "Religious Instruction: Homemaking," in *Mapping Christian Education: Approaches to Congregational Learning,* ed. Jack Seymour (Nashville: Abingdon, 1997), 88.

2. Parenting for Faith Expression

1. Ellen T. Charry, "Raising Christian Children in a Pagan Culture," *Christian Century,* February 16, 1994, 166.

2. Caldwell, "Religious Instruction: Homemaking," 87.

3. Hulda Niebuhr, "Parental Education in the Church," *International Journal of Religious Education* 6, no. 1 (October 1929): 13.

4. Ibid.

5. Huebner, "Christian Growth in Faith," 516–17.

6. Mark Searle, "Infant Baptism Reconsidered," in *Alternative Futures for Worship,* vol. 2, *Baptism and Confirmation* (Collegeville, Minn.: Liturgical Press, 1987), 48–49.

7. Gellman, *God's Mailbox,* xi, xii.

8. Ibid.

9. Madeleine L'Engle, *Two-Part Invention: The Story of a Marriage* (New York: Farrar, Straus & Giroux, 1988), 125.

10. Huebner, "Christian Growth in Faith," 515.

11. Ibid.

12. *Growing in the Life of Christian Faith* (Louisville: Presbyterian Church [USA], 1989), iv.

13. Ibid., v.

14. Ibid., 28.

15. Charles Foster relates this story in his book *Educating Congregations,* 52.

16. Robert Coles, *The Moral Intelligence of Children* (New York: Random House, 1997), 31.

17. Thanks to Cathy Hoop for sharing this story with me about a workshop she offered for parents at Second Presbyterian Church in Nashville, Tennessee.

18. Barbara Brown Taylor used this image in her book *Bread of Angels* (Boston: Cowley Publications, 1997), 11.

19. Elizabeth F. Caldwell, *Come Unto Me: Rethinking the Sacraments for Children* (Cleveland: United Church Press, 1996), 85.

20. Taylor, *Bread of Angels,* 10.

21. Mary Pipher, *The Shelter of Each Other: Rebuilding Our Families* (New York: Grosset/Putnam, 1996), 7.

22. Ibid., 230.

23. Ibid., 245.

24. John Westerhoff, *Bringing Up Children in the Christian Faith* (San Francisco: Harper & Row, 1980), 37.

25. Ibid., 44.

26. Ibid., 49.

27. Ibid.

28. Ibid., 51.

29. Searle, "Infant Baptism Reconsidered," 47.

30. David B. Batchelder, "The Home as Family Church," *Reformed Liturgy and Music* 29, no. 3 (Louisville: Presbyterian Church [USA], 1995): 168.

31. Pipher, *The Shelter of Each Other,* 59.

32. Tom F. Driver, *The Magic of Ritual: Our Need for Liberating Rites That Transform Our Lives and Our Communities* (San Francisco: HarperSanFrancisco, 1991), 4–5.

33. Ibid., 131. I commend this book for its potential to stimulate thinking in new ways about ritual and worship in our lives.

34. Ibid.

35. Ibid., 124.

36. For more reading on the function that order brings to ritual, see Roy A. Rapport, *Ecology, Meaning, and Religion* (Berkeley, Calif.: North Atlantic Books, 1979).

3. Imprints of Faith

1. I am grateful to my sister, Cathy Caldwell Hoop, director of children's ministries at Second Presbyterian Church in Nashville, for sharing the quotes of children used at the beginning of some sections of this chapter.

2. Kathleen Norris, *Dakota* (New York: Ticknor & Fields, 1993), 2.

3. Kathleen Norris, *Cloister Walk* (New York: Riverhead Books, 1996), 59.

4. Ibid., 60.

5. Ibid., 64.

6. Ibid.

7. Ibid.

8. Thanks to my father, William Pitts Caldwell, for sharing this story about my baptism in May of 1948.

9. Jean Grasso Fitzpatrick, *Something More: Nurturing Your Child's Spiritual Growth* (New York: Viking, 1991), 44.

10. Ibid., 47.

11. For additional reading on developmental theory as it pertains to the growth of children and adolescents, see Jean Piaget (cognitive development), Erik Erikson (psychological/social development), Lawrence Kohlberg (moral development), and James Fowler (faith development). The work of Carol Gilligan in her book *In a Different Voice* and her more recent research into the development of girls add an important voice to the work of the classical developmental theorists. Two additional theorists who are making significant contributions to our understanding of human development are Robert Kegan in *The Evolving Self* (Cambridge: Harvard University Press, 1982) and Daniel N. Stern in *The Interpersonal World of the Infant* (New York: Basic Books, 1985).

12. Edith Hunter, *Sophia Lyon Fahs* (Boston: Beacon Press, 1976), 173.

13. James W. Fowler, "Strength for the Journey: Early Childhood Development in Selfhood and Faith," in *Faith Development in Early Childhood,* ed. Doris A. Blazer (Kansas City, Mo.: Sheed and Ward, 1989), 30.

14. Thanks to my friend Marianne Rhebergen for sharing this story about her daughter, Kristin.

15. See John Westerhoff, *Bringing Up Children in the Christian Faith.* The last stage in Westerhoff's pilgrimage of faith is a mature faith, associated with adults. The concepts Westerhoff identifies are more fully described in James Fowler, *Stages of Faith: The Psychology of Human Development and the Quest for Meaning* (San Francisco: Harper & Row, 1981).

16. Kegan, *The Evolving Self,* 121.

17. "'Is this Nativity?' Elementary Fellowship Visits Second Harvest Food Bank," *Second Story,* newsletter of Second Presbyterian Church, Nashville, Tennessee, January 1997.

18. *10 Things Every Child Needs,* WTTW Productions, Chicago, Illinois, April 1997.

19. Thanks to John Buchanan, pastor, Fourth Presbyterian Church, Chicago, for sharing this story with me.

20. Cited in Fitzpatrick, *Something More,* 134.

21. Ibid.

22. An excellent resource for learning about prayer is Richard Foster, *Prayer: Finding the Heart's True Home* (San Francisco: HarperSanFrancisco, 1992).

23. This quality is taken from a description of a household's commitment to living a life of faith in Caldwell, *Come Unto Me,* 114–16.

24. Maria Harris, *The Faith of Parents* (New York: Paulist Press, 1991), 27.

25. Sandy Eisenberg Sasso, *In God's Name* (Woodstock, Vt.: Jewish Lights Publishing, 1994). Another excellent book for considering names and images of God in the Bible is by John and Katherine Paterson, *Images of God* (New York: Clarion Books, 1998).

26. Marc Gellman and Thomas Hartman, *Where Does God Live? Questions and Answers for Parents and Children* (New York: Triumph Books, 1991), 19–22.

27. Reeve Lindbergh, *The Circle of Days* (Cambridge, Mass.: Candlewick Press, 1998).

4. "And When Your Child Asks"

1. Sylvia Ann Hewlett and Cornel West, *The War against Parents: What We Can Do for America's Beleaguered Moms and Dads* (New York: Houghton Mifflin, 1998), 153.

2. Barbara Kimes Myers and William R. Myers, *Engaging in Transcendence: The Church's Ministry and Covenant with Young Children* (Cleveland: The Pilgrim Press, 1992), 139.

3. Ibid.

4. For additional reading in psychosocial development see Erik Erikson, *Childhood and Society,* 2d ed. (New York: Norton, 1963).

5. James Fowler, "The Public Church: Ecology for Faith Education and Advocate for Children," in *Faith Development in Early Childhood,* 140.

6. Gellman and Hartman, *Where Does God Live?,* 13.

7. Harold S. Kushner, *When Children Ask about God: A Guide for Parents Who Don't Always Have All the Answers* (New York: Schocken Books, 1989), xiv.

8. Many excellent books provide an introduction to the basic tenets of Christian faith. Theologians in the last twenty years have added their perspective on Christian theology from feminist, womanist, Asian, African American, and liberation perspectives. I have chosen to work with a text originally written for use by adults in church school classes. I commend this book in its revised edition to you for additional reading and study: Shirley C. Guthrie, *Christian Doctrine* (Louisville: Westminster/John Knox Press, 1994), 9.

9. Ibid., 5.

10. Nancy White Carlstrom, *Does God Know How to Tie Shoes?* (Grand Rapids, Mich.: Eerdmans, 1993), 4.

11. Sasso, *In God's Name,* 5.

12. Ibid., 31.

13. Guthrie, *Christian Doctrine,* 54.

14. Ibid.

15. Nancy Sohn Swartz, *In Our Image: God's First Creatures* (Woodstock, Vt.: Jewish Lights Publishing, 1998), 26.

16. Guthrie, *Christian Doctrine,* vi, vii.

17. This is Guthrie's definition of providence, ibid., 166.

18. Ibid., 213.

19. Ibid., 221.

20. Lois Rock, *The Gentle Carpenter* (Colorado Springs: Lion Publishing, 1997).

21. Guthrie, *Christian Doctrine,* 259.

22. Ibid.

23. These words from children are included in Children of America, *The 11th Commandment: Wisdom from Our Children* (Woodstock, Vt.: Jewish Lights Publishing, 1996).

24. Guthrie, *Christian Doctrine,* 319.

25. Ibid., 323.

26. Ibid., 331–32.

27. "We Are the Church," words and music by Richard Avery and Donald Marsh, Proclamation Productions, Inc., Port Jervis, New York.

28. Marc Gellman and Thomas Hartman, *How Do You Spell God? Answers to the Big Questions from Around the World* (New York: Morrow Junior Books, 1995), 145–46.

29. This form was originally printed as "Biblical Themes in Primary Terms" in a teacher's resource book for kindergarten teachers, written by Pauline Palmer Meek in the *Discovering the Bible with Children Series 5,* no. 1 (Valley Forge, Pa.: Sept., Oct., Nov. 1980). This resource was part of a cooperative curriculum project of the 1970s called Joint Educational Development.

30. The Alternatives Resource Center has been developing curricular resources for use at home and at church for many years. These are the titles from Advent and lenten studies. The focus of the educational materials is on living simply and faithfully in the world. The curricular resources for Advent and Lent have particular emphasis on the religious celebration of these holidays as opposed to cultural expectations. For more information, contact Alternatives for Simple Living, P.O. Box 2857, Sioux City, IA 51106, 1-800-821-6153. The Web address is www.SimpleLiving.org.

31. For more detailed help with teaching about the sacraments with children, see Caldwell, *Come Unto Me.*

32. These questions are chapter titles used by Gellman and Hartman in their book *How Do You Spell God?.*

33. Marjorie Thompson, *Family as the Forming Center: A Vision of the Role of Family in Spiritual Formation* (Nashville: Upper Room Books, 1996), 15.

34. See Jacqueline L. Tobin and Raymond G. Dobard, *Hidden in Plain View: A Secret Story of Quilts and the Underground Railroad* (New York: Doubleday, 1999).

35. Patricia Polacco, *The Keeping Quilt* (New York: Simon & Schuster, 1988).

5. A Faithful Ecology at Home, at Church, and in the World

1. This term has been used as a way to describe a network of both institutional and individual practices and commitments that together nurture the life of the Christian in the world. See "The Ecology for Nurturing Faith: Education, Disciplines, and Programs for Faith Development," in Milton J. Coalter, John M. Mulder, and Louis B. Weeks, *The Re-Forming Tradition: Presbyterians and Mainstream Protestantism* (Louisville: Westminster/John Knox, 1992).

2. James Fowler speaks about the public church as ecology for faith education and the importance of all the generations being present to tell the stories of faith. See James Fowler, "The Public Church."

3. Ibid., 145.

4. Maya Angelou, *Wouldn't Take Nothing for My Journey Now* (New York: Random House, 1993), 74.

5. Westerhoff, *Bringing Up Children in the Christian Faith,* 72.

6. Searle, "Infant Baptism Reconsidered," 47.

7. *Book of Common Worship* (Louisville: Westminster/John Knox Press, 1993), 406.

8. In his book *Educating Congregations,* Charles Foster has identified the role and place of children in congregational life. He is concerned that in some educational activities with children, there is more focus on performance than on building relationships across the generations.

9. Walter Brueggemann, "The Family as World-Maker," *Journal for Preachers* 7 (Easter 1985): 8.

10. Harris, *The Faith of Parents,* 16–19.

11. Ibid., 17–18.

12. Ibid., 18.

13. Nelson, *Where Faith Begins,* 10.

14. Westerhoff, *Will Our Children Have Faith?,* 126.

15. Myers and Myers, *Engaging in Transcendence,* 94.

16. Ibid., 21.

17. The Children's Defense Fund in Washington, D.C., has been providing educational resources and liturgy for use in educating Protestant, Jewish, and Catholic congregations about the realities and potential for children in our culture. The packet of resources made available each summer can be ordered from 215 E. Street, N.W., Washington, DC 20001, 202-628-8787, or visit the Web site at www.childrensdefense.org.

18. This is just one story of a faithful congregation that models the core conditions for ministry with all of God's people. It is the Pullen Memorial Baptist Church of Raleigh, North Carolina.

19. Deborah Alberswerth Payden and Laura Loving, *Celebrating at Home: Prayers and Liturgies for Families* (Cleveland: United Church Press, 1998), xi.

20. Many Protestant churches participate in an offering for the One Great Hour of Sharing, which supports disaster relief, refugee resettlement, and the development of rural and urban communities throughout the United States and the world.

21. Maria Harris, *Proclaim Jubilee! A Spirituality for the Twenty-first Century* (Louisville: Westminster/John Knox Press, 1996), 29, 27.

22. Ibid., 75.

23. Westerhoff, *Bringing Up Children in the Christian Faith,* 26.

24. One of the best sources for children's bulletins that are coordinated with the lectionary texts is the *Peace Papers,* available from Parenting for Peace and Justice Network; E-mail address: ppjn@aol.com. In addition to activities for children, there is a family page.

25. For more reading in the theory of multiple intelligences that focuses on seven intelligences (linguistic, logical-mathematical, spatial, bodily-kinesthetic, musical, interpersonal, and intrapersonal), see Thomas Armstrong, *Multiple Intelligences in the Classroom* (Alexandria, Va.: Association for Supervision and Curriculum Development, 1994), or Howard Gardner, *Frames of Mind: The Theory of Multiple Intelligences* (New York: Basic Books, 1983).

Appendix 1

1. Used by permission of Kirsten Stangenes and Allison Denny, members of Lincoln Park Presbyterian Church, Chicago, Illinois.

Appendix 3

1. Thomas Boomershine, *Story Journey: An Invitation to the Gospel as Storytelling* (Nashville: Abingdon, 1988), 20.

2. Ibid., 28.

3. Ibid., 36.